D0909083

Pearlman Memorial Library
Central Bible Institute
Springfield, Missouri

THE STORY OF THE CHRISTIAN YEAR

The
STORY
of the
CHRISTIAN YEAR

by

GEORGE M. GIBSON

Illustrated by the Author

18330

New York

ABINGDON-COKESBURY PRESS

Nashville

Pearlman Memorial Library
Central Bible Institute
Springfield, Missouri

THE STORY OF THE CHRISTIAN YEAR

COPYRIGHT, MCMXLV
By WHITMORE & STONE

All rights in this book are reserved. No part of the text
may be reproduced in any form without written permission of the publishers, except brief quotations used
in connection with reviews in magazines or newspapers.

K
Printed in U. S. A.

To

BETTY and MORGAN

for

Comradeship and

Encouragement

FOREWORD

The Reasons for This Writing

I am no formalist in religion; I was digged from the pit of liberal Protestantism. "The religion of the spirit" moves me more than all religions of authority. Though these be hard days for free faith and practice, I continue growth in that belief which, almost from the cradle, has remained the center of changing convictions—a belief in the free God moving upon the spirits of men through the free Christ, to bring them into full liberty of redemption.

Indeed it is a zeal for this very liberty which has moved me these late years to a deepening experience of the disciplines which are the true conditions of freedom. How many of the moderns have confessed to the dialectic of untaught and unprincipled liberty which carried in itself the seeds of slavery! Such confessions have marked an entire literary epoch, furnishing the theme of a large production of writing. Thomas Wolfe and Aldous Huxley, Archibald MacLeish and T. S. Eliot have this confession in common, though they meet the new situation in various ways and approach salvation in different degrees. Jointly they cry the lost soul of a modern age that took liberty for an absolute value and turned religious liberty particularly into a negation of itself.

Since all religions make a point of disciplinary practice, this mood of the times may indicate a renewed interest in religion itself as well as its forms. The very idea of rule and routine was but a little while ago repellent to most Americans, and was regarded by Protestants as the trap of authoritarianism. We may now, to be sure, look for spurious applica-

7

tions of discipline. An age grown tired, all but exhausted, with its license may cry out, "Give us a king!" At any rate, false claimants will show themselves, false persons and deceitful philosophies, seeking to capitalize upon the social preparedness for discipline.

But the times are also favorable for such as will seek the rigorous correction of their souls by means which are at once classic and sensitive to new demands. Every life aim carries its peculiar requirements for the techniques of its accomplishment, and those who have taken as supreme goal the glorification of God have shown a remarkable unity in their devotional practices. William James could write of *The Varieties of Religious Experience,* drawing most of his materials from the more experimental forms of faith; but one could also enter a convincing catalogue of facts supporting the theme "The Unity of Religious Experience," for the saints in far separate centuries and in lands as wide apart as the earth have, through a common commitment to Christ, found a common means toward a glorious fulfillment.

For the broad culture of Protestant Christianity, as well as for guidance in the personal religious life, I have drawn together this volume. It issues, not from personal experience alone, but from the collective experience of our historic Christianity. And perhaps our having held its subject matter in light regard the past few centuries has some bearing upon the religious illiteracy and unfaith of the masses, so much bewailed today in professional religious circles.

Protestantism needs the unity of cultural and spiritual practice which a rediscovery of the Christian Year will give it. The proposal is bold, considering the continuing suspicion of religious subjectivists toward all forms and observances. But it is also timely, having been anticipated by a general interest in the unified practices called for by a common faith. The ecumenical consciousness not only modifies former suspicions but quickens sympathetic interest in the usages of all branches of the Church universal, and in the contribution of each part to the growing tradition of the whole. Hence this book is offered. There is no compulsion for the adoption of all the suggestions of the Ecclesiastical Year; the author himself puts it to no slavish use. A great deal of its material is of interest to Protestants mainly as history, and some of its features are entirely outside Protestant acceptance. Discrimination is necessary, though the individual may be assisted by various denominational and interchurch guides. It is in that spirit that this book is offered. It is without ecclesiastical authority, its suggestions resting upon such truth and timeliness as they may contain. It is hoped that this study may prove an aid in three particular ways:

As a help to the minister in planning his preaching, worship, and correlated activities of parish administration;

As a means of grace to the individual Christian who strives to make his personal devotional life vital through regularity, direction, content, and relationship with the total fellowship;

And as a contribution to that general Christian unity which we seek today along many lines, and in which we place our hope for a redeemed world. Observance of the practices of a common culture is one of the products of ecumenicity.

Acknowledgments and Apologies

To all the saints and all the souls of the past twenty centuries from whose heroic and devoted lives the Christian Year has evolved I express honest thanks for help and inspiration in this and every good work.

Further acknowledgment is due my contemporaries who, in their books, sermons, and group discussions, are expressing a vital interest in the classic "core of the ages" and a sensitivity to the "great tradition."

A very special mention must be made of the United Church of Hyde Park which by its rare combination of experimental faith and reverence for the churchly tradition has offered a stimulus for this study and a field for its application. Mr. Philip Manuel, director of music, with unusual gifts of liturgical insight as well as musicianship, is largely responsible for the beauty and reality of our worship, and has been of invaluable aid to me personally in this work. Mrs. Philip L. Mathisen, director of religious education and pageantry, makes a most excellent use of the living arts in the celebrations of our fellowship. The faculty under her leadership sat with me for a long semester in the Christian Year, and aided in gathering materials for this book.

Finally, abundant thanks to my wife, Elizabeth Leeper Gibson, and son Morgan, who gave me daily encouragement to make a book of what I had discovered about these ceremonials, and who, by sympathetic interest, helped to bring it to completion. Without their inspiration it would most likely not have been accomplished.

As a footnote to these expressions of thanks I address a word of apology to the fraternity of Christian scholarship for the errors and omissions that have no doubt crept into the manuscript. Such a book as this takes one into many specialized fields without a specialist's equipment. I can no more than appeal for the leniency of those in whose life vocations I am an amateur, and shall appreciate their criticisms for possible future corrections.

GEORGE M. GIBSON

CONTENTS

I. TIME AND MAN   15

The origin in nature—observances as social history—the
time sense: the day; the week; the month; the season; and
the year—the historic sense—*sub specie aeternitatis*—the
founding of calendars

II. THE JEWISH CEREMONIAL YEAR   40

The Jewish calendar—the ceremonies—the Sabbath—the
New Year—the Day of Atonement—the Feast of Tabernacles—the Feast of Lights—the Feast of Lots—the Passover—Pentecost—prophets and psalmists

III. THE CELEBRATIONS OF PAGAN ROME   56

The Roman calendar—the pagan celebrations

IV. NEW TESTAMENT BEGINNINGS   68

Origin of the Christian Year—Passover to Eucharist—
Sabbath to Sunday—principles of form—four guiding
principles: reiteration; appropriateness; separation;
preparation

V. CEREMONIAL ELABORATION   79

Easter and days dependent—Pentecost—Ascension Day—
the Epiphany—Christmas—the determination of times—
the principle of preparation and the joining of seasons—
fasting and feasting—the principle of separation and the
conflict of cultures—the Easter controversy and the
Council of Nicaea—saints' days

VI. CONQUEST AND CONVERSION   107

Christian universalism—barbarians—symbols and ceremonies as means of grace—the missionary spread—new
idolatry for old—credulous worship of saints and Mary—
—East and West—new additions

VII. CORRUPTIONS AND ADORNMENTS   124

Crusades foster superstitions—the Ecclesiastical Year
mothers literature and drama—the decisive century—
clericos laicos

. VIII. AWAKENING AND REFORM   133

Renaissance and Reformation—shadows of coming events
—faith and merit—Continental reform within the ceremonial practices—Luther—Zwingli—Farel and Calvin

IX. THE CHRISTIAN YEAR IN ENGLISH
PROTESTANTISM   143

Chaucer—the Monk of Malvern—indigenous reform movement—the break of Henry VIII—Somerset seeks uniformity—Mary returns to Romanism—Elizabeth restores independent church—wide popular use of the Christian Year
—reinterpretations and latitudinarianism—forced unity
under James and Charles—Puritanism and the "Sabbath"
—Dissenters and Separatists abolish times and seasons—
two centuries of conflict

X. THE CHRISTIAN YEAR IN AMERICA   163

Religious motive for colonization—first extensions by ceremonial religion—Colonial Protestantism the determining
culture—Reformist suspicion of form—local celebrations
and observances begin—the Revolution—the classical
minority—religious movements—French anticlericalism
and the antireligious temper—American religious motive
in the informal tradition—liberal Protestantism and ecclesiastical usage—development of new and restoration of old

CONTENTS

XI. THE PRESENT PROSPECT   177

    Secularism overwhelms the sanctities—planless anarchism
—influences for the revival of the Christian Year—more
preparation—civil calendar reform

XII. VALUES OF AN ORDERED CALENDAR   187

    The whole gospel—Christian doctrine—ecumenical wor-
ship—Bible reading—the historic sense—religious education—long-range planning—personal and social needs—
the year as a whole

ALL THE SUNDAYS IN THE YEAR   205

CALENDAR OF FIXED DAYS   222

SELECTED BIBLIOGRAPHY   229

INDEX   231

Chapter I

TIME AND MAN

IT happens that this writing begins in the month of September, so named as the seventh month of the Martial year. To one conscious of the calendar, the month is full of special significances. Great events and great personalities come up from the past to remind him of those values he would be prone to neglect; and once more the turning cycle of time brings before his consciousness a consideration of particular duties and privileges of Christian thought and life. In this regard September is no different from any other part of the year. At whatever time period we find ourselves, there are these special and particular emphases, as illustrated by the current month.

Here we are, by the very name of the calendar division, reminded of the Roman paganism into which Christianity entered as an obscure sect, then passed from obscurity into persecution and finally into triumph. Here begins autumn,

> Heralded by the rain
> With banners, by great gales incessant fanned,

recalling the natural aspect of religion in the order of creation. This is an American month, marking the passage of the Constitution and the recognition of our independence by England. It is the month of the National Anthem, the preliminary Negro Emancipation Proclamation, Labor Day, and other national days, all recalling how the historic Christian culture offers the generous ground for the growth

15

of free and just political institutions. The Jewish New Year and the feasts of Atonement and Tabernacles invite the celebration of Christianity's more antique origins, and further cultivation of the relationship of creative good will with those of our mother faith. Great personalities are present in this month, Christians as far removed from each other in time as Paul, Chrysostom, Cyprian, Jerome, Wenceslaus. And over all it is one of the months of Kingdomtide, in the second half of the Church Year, which is called the Season of Trinity.

The Origin in Nature

Any month taken from the calendar at random would offer a similar series of meanings, and would illustrate how that most mysterious phenomenon of nature, time, enters into the practical lives of men and of national cultures. To understand the real origin of the Christian Year would be to understand the nature of time itself, and the effort would move through history into metaphysics. Thus, Richard Hooker begins his account of Christian practices with a survey of the order of God's creation, and finds in the movements of seasons and the rhythms of all physical structures God's own decision as to the particular worths of separate times and occurrences. This Christian conception of the divine purpose as revealed in constant recurrence is quite different from the pagan notion of the meaninglessness of ceaseless change. "Time," wrote Marcus Aurelius, one of the noblest Romans, "is a sort of river of passing events, and strong is its current. No sooner is a thing brought to sight than it is swept by and another takes its place; and this too will be swept away."

But Jewish-Christian thought is more impressed with the constant reiterations of nature and history, and with their revelation of the Creator, than with the idea of ceaseless change. The Genesis account of the origin of all things in God has not omitted the circular motion of the universe as part of his handiwork, nor failed to imply the divine intention to order all things in seasonal recurrence. From the individual's alternations of energy and fatigue, hunger and satisfaction, and the rhythms of all bodily functions, through tides, seasons, and years, not forgetting the major climacterics of history, the constant reiterations of creation are as notable as its change. That "history always repeats itself" is as true as the opposite adage, that it never does. "Time," wrote Hooker, "is the measure of the motion of heaven, so that we must of necessity use the benefit of years, days, hours, minutes, which all grow from the celestial motion. . . . Circular motion and uniform celerity must needs touch often at the same points; they cannot choose but to bring unto us by equal distances frequent returns of the same times."

Observances as Social History

Common to all cultures is the association of events to their proper times and places, with fitting observances. All peoples have their calendars; they are not entirely invented, but grow out of the common stream of life, revealing the inner soul of each separate culture. Whether with the ancient Romans making orgies at Saturnalia, or the Chinese as described by Pearl Buck hailing the New Year with mirth, gifts, and confetti, or in ancient Babylon or contemporary America, the inner life of folk is read in their outward observances. For people celebrate what they deem to have worth; their cultures are the embodiment and form they give to values, whether consciously or unconsciously accepted. "Festivals have preeminently a social character and express the feelings of an entire community, whether clan, tribe, or nation. Being folk possessions, they are very tenacious of life, and may exist through long ages almost unchanged in nature." [1]

And the soul of culture is worship, the celebration of that

---

[1] Webster Hutton in *Dictionary of Religion and Ethics* (New York: The Macmillan Co., 1921).

Highest Value considered worthy of supreme devotion and most genuine service.

So calendar making is a growth of social experience as well as a study of the natural celestial order. John Selden, distinguished seventeenth-century layman, answered the antiformal movement of his time by trying to show that the Dissenters indeed revolted against a particular formality, namely that called "popery," rather than against the reality of form itself. Protestantism and, in fact, all sound religions of the spirit are right in assigning less than first place to outward observances. But the implication that a formless faith, making no deposit upon the common culture mode, is automatically superior to one that expresses itself in liturgies and rites is based upon a false assumption. The deceiving assumption is that these "outward signs of an inward grace" are mere inventions of men, and that they may therefore be dispensed with upon man's own motion. Havelock Ellis in *The Dance of Life* saw the deeper meanings of rites and celebrations, saying, "the Mass is of nature," although he was no devotee of the Church.

The spirit must express itself in form; one may as well speak of an artist so pure as never to paint a picture, as of a religion so spiritual, universal, and absolute as to find no suitable expression in particular times and places. Given a vital spirit, the form will follow as the fruit the vine; and they are as wrong who think the spirit is sufficient without form as those who would have form without spirit. All efforts to be once and for all rid of outward paraphernalia of religion simply result in the end in the production of other paraphernalia, or a loss of the movement in total secularization. The very formlessness becomes formal; the silences themselves become fraught with symbolism.

So the outward modes of a society reveal its inner spirit. Selden sees the picture of a whole age in the pictorial concreteness of rites:

18

There is no Church without a Liturgy, nor indeed can there be conveniently, as there is no School without a Grammar. One Scholar may be taught otherwise upon the Stock of his Acumen, but not the whole School. One or two that are piously disposed may serve themselves in their own way, but hardly a whole Nation. . . .

To know what was generally believed in all Ages, the way is to consult the Liturgies, not any man's private Writing. As if you should know how the Church of England serves God, go to the Common Prayer-Book, consult not this or that Man. Besides, Liturgies never compliment, nor use high Expressions. The Fathers at times speak oratoriously.[2]

As social history is recorded in the calendar of a nation or a religion, the practice of observances and liturgies by the faithful is a social experience, offering emancipation from egoistic superiority and separation, which is religion's chief enemy. One's private devotions and public worship bring the healing of humility as he discovers himself part of a vast fellowship engaged through the ages and across the world in the same confession and dramatizing supreme loyalty by a common means. One is only a part of that fellowship; hence the willful assertions of self are subdued. Yet he is part, and his soul's significance is enlarged by the supporting cloud of witnesses.

So the Church Year grows from the ground of nature and upward through the common experience. Its Christianity does not consist in its being a mere calendar, but in that it elevates into daily custom the great events and persons centering around Christ as satellites around their Star.

The Time Sense: The Day

Man's time sense is one key to his intellectual and spiritual growth, and to the development of his civilizations. He lives at the center of an area of effective events, of occurrences which enter into his conscious experience and offer the basis

[2] *Table Talk* (Dutton ed.), p. 49.

for his living. The time awareness of the child or the primitive goes little beyond the unit of the day. The rhythm of sleeping and waking, eating and resting, makes up his life. He lives so completely in the present that days past are almost indistinguishable from days to come. "Yesterday" and "tomorrow" are interchangeable terms to the child.

Primitives, like children, have little conception of time. Yet even in the least developed peoples rites and celebrations  are discovered in amazing intricacy and persistence. If set times are followed, it is seemingly by a mass instinct rather than by design. Stuart Chase has noted among the more primitive villages of Mexico how the fiestas and other public affairs go forward as though by a common consent rather than by planning. There are no committees. No one can give the time-conscious American any satisfaction as to when or where the various features of the celebration will be. Yet, as though by instinct, just as birds know when to migrate or bees to swarm, the villagers gather and the rites begin, each automatically taking his place in the music, the dancing, or the sacrifices.

While the deep unconscious social possession is large, the conscious life of the primitive individual is of a narrow scope. He is a creature of a day so far as concerns the major events of his life. The course of the sun from dawn to dark and the creep of the shadows across the ground offer the cosmic setting for the movements of his own person by the instincts and habits that control him. Larger divisions of time are vaguely beyond his effective  area; he knows no historic past nor prophetic future. Likewise the lesser divisions, of such importance to modern man, are of unimportance to him. Man is well along in his civilizations before seconds and minutes are of much value to him, and even with the ancient Jews and Babylonians the hours were inexact in comparison to our own. Their days were divided into large, rough, but usable chunks adapted to the requirements of simple living. "Morning," "heat of the day," and "cool of the day" were convenient enough for the usual pursuits of the day; and for nights, uneventful except for possible attack, the "first," "middle," and "morning watches" sufficed. From earliest times on through history this primary unit in man's time measurement was honored in legend and song. The Jews included it in the creation story: "And God divided the light from the darkness. And God called the light *Day,* and the darkness he called *Night.* And the evening and the morning were the first day."

This is the natural day, or the light time, which varies with the season of the year. The calendar day of exactly twenty-four hours comes much later. There is also the civil day, established by law or custom, which varies from culture to culture. Thus the Hebrews measured from one sunset to the next, the Babylonians from sunrise to sunrise; some measured from noon to noon, and others from midnight to midnight.

The Week

The week has no precise natural origin, though there is a rough correspondence to the phases of the moon. It was of magical and later of religious significance, and yet later was incorporated fully into the social scheme. Earth and the heavenly bodies have no regular weekly assignment, but the number seven took on a mystic meaning which is found in all the Eastern peoples as far back as they are studied; and the week is an institution at first peculiar to these peoples. It is to be found in the calendars of the Brahmins of India. The Babylonians marked the seventh, fourteenth, twenty-first, and twenty-eighth days of two of their months as days of penitence. The Jews gave it a religious meaning in the crea-ation story, as did the Chaldeans; and the Jewish Sabbath, marking the rest day at the end of the week, scored off time into these exact subdivisions convenient as well for vocational and civic purposes as for religious observances. The week was not in Greek or Roman thinking, although the latter came to use the term Sabbath and accept the week as a contribution from the Jews. Although there are references to its use in the time of Severus in the third century A.D., it was not until Theodosius in the fourth that it appears fully incorporated into the Roman scheme.

Many current customs are traceable to magical origins, the customs remaining after the magic is no longer believed, being reinterpreted in the light of social and religious development. The ancient numerologies linger with us yet and confer special meanings on religion, the arts, and social customs. Threes, fives, sevens, and twelves are especially notable in this regard. And thus the week, beginning with the ancient taboos around the number seven, grows to become an indispensable unit of civil and religious calendars, and is justified in terms of the need of the human body for one day's rest in seven. In the present names of the days of the week we see the influence of other cultures upon our own, three of the days being traceable back through the North European culture to the heavenly bodies — the Day of the Sun, the Day of the Moon, and the Day of Saturn—and four being the Scandinavian equivalents of Roman deities: Tiw, god of war; Woden, the chief deity, god of air and sky and giver of fruits; Thor, or Donor, god of thunder and weather; and Freya, or Fro, goddess of love. The Roman week was: *Dies Solis, Lunae, Martis, Mercurii, Jovis, Veneris, Saturni,* showing the planetary influence.

The "octave" is a term which came much later into the Christian calendar, sometimes meaning the eight-day period from any festival to its next Sunday, inclusive. In other uses the octave refers only to the eighth day rather than to the full period of eight days. This unit of measurement is not used outside the religious calendar.

The Month

With growth and agricultural experience comes the sense of the month. With early man the year still seems an eternity, as his simple life is without such occasions as would mark off the longer division of time. From the vantage point of the year end, the year's beginning would seem an antiquity away, and the next year end would seem a future as infinitely removed as the child's expectation of the coming Christmas. It was quite natural that the month should be discovered before the year, and that the earliest calendars should therefore be lunar rather than solar. And while much guesswork attached to the first efforts to "reduce the year to better reckoning," the significant point is that man was making an effort to observe objective facts rather than merely inventing artificial conveniences. The month is a natural division, marked from new moon to new moon, and related to such earthly phenomena as the tides of the sea and the rhythms of the human body, more particularly in the female. Greeks, Romans, Babylonians, Chinese, Persians, as well as the Hebrews, all constructed their calendars upon the principle of lunar rotation. With the Jews each separate month was established by actual observation by witnesses of the rise of the new moon

over the horizon of the sea and by report of these witnesses to the court, which thereupon confirmed it. Announcement of the new month was made by a blast of the shophar. Our present months are no longer identical with the moons because of later accommodation to the solar year.

As the calendar grows through social experience, each separate month takes on its own character and accumulates meaning through legend and use.

The Season

The season, being a natural and beautiful division of time, is noted even among primitives. So marked are the passages between seasons they would hardly escape notice even among people with a very limited time sense. And so deep are the season's influences upon the world life—plant, animal, and human—that the meanings are noted in terms of fertility, birth, death, and decay, the major movements in the dance of life. All calendars show this seasonal influence, the civil and religious celebrations in all lands reiterating the times of planting and harvest, winter and summer. Besides the major seasonal festivals, the Christian calendar observes the Ember days and weeks at each season's beginning, during which special blessings upon the functions of the particular season

24

are sought. This custom is in direct succession of agricultural rites of the very earliest peoples. Every aspect of crop cultivation was given ceremonial attention, from the preparation of the soil to the final ingathering; and eventualities, such as drought, were also occasions of special rites. The most elaborate system of seasonal observances, according to Dr. A. Eustace Haydon, is in China, where the state religion directs every imaginable agricultural rite. The superstitious motives of primitive and pagan religions are transcended in Christianity by the teaching of the providence of God.

The word "season" means "planting time," and indicates the outstanding agricultural need from which the concept arose. There followed the other natural divisions, each sharply marked off from the preceding by a prevailing type of weather and specialized demands in agricultural work. Astronomical development later discovered the objective basis for the seasons in the tilt of the earth's axis and the relative distance of its poles from the sun. The seasonal beginnings came to be marked by the sun's passage successively into the signs of Aries, Libra, Cancer, and Capricornus. Certain sections of the world have three seasons, dry, wet, and cold; still others have only two, dry and wet. The Vedic Indians had six: flowery, hot, rainy, sultry, frosty, and dewy. Our seasons are: spring, beginning at the vernal equinox on March 21; summer, at the summer solstice on June 21; autumn, at the autumnal equinox, September 23; and winter, at the winter solstice, December 21.

With the growth of the Christian Year the term "season" was applied to any stretch of time devoted to one religious purpose, such as "the season of Lent," "Advent season," or "Epiphany season."

Throughout, this growing time sense is accompanied by religious awakenings. Crude notions of divinity are enlarged toward the providence of the Creator God who, "as the swift seasons roll," orders all things rightly and requires the duties of the faithful to be performed "in his season from year to year."

And the Year

The unit of the year is a discovery of a higher astronomical order, being the time required for the apparent movement of the sun around the ecliptic, or of the earth around the sun. A primitive would hardly know what an advanced astronomy would later discover, that that time period amounts to exactly 365 days, 5 hours, 48 minutes, and 45.51 seconds. The natural compass of early man's effective events would be measured by

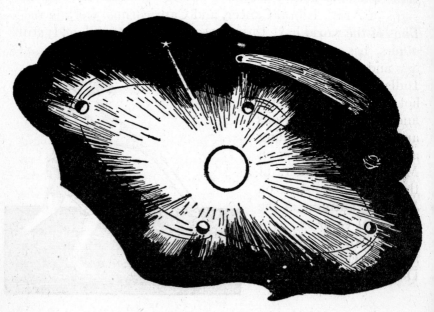

a very few moons before and after his present moment. So the first years were rough groupings of months, or moons, inexactly ranging from five to twelve, and meaning little more than "a longer time than usual." Yet even before the full use of solar calendars, the moon year had become fairly well established and of a length approximating the sun year. The difficulty of adjustment between the old moon calendars and the sun year resulted in a mixture of methods, and we still have in our present Christian Year both means of computation, Easter and dates dependent upon it being movable according to the moon, while Christmas and other dates are fixed on the solar calendar. Some time schemes were tried by the exact division of the sun year into twelfths of the total distance around the zodiac. It is interesting to note that while the whole Eastern world was still using the moon as its chief time marker, the American primitives were even then following the sun. Solstitial ceremonies are still held among the Pueblo Indians, and the famous Aztec calendar stone in Mexico City is a sun calendar.

The Historic Sense

It is only with maturity and civilization that the historic sense is born, extending the area of effective events to include years, quadrenia, decades, and even centuries and eras. Yet even in a civilization as highly developed as ours today "average men" still live in a very limited time area. They scorn the thought that century-old events have any instructive bearing upon the present, and are apt to forget between wars, or even between political campaigns, the most important things those occasions would have to teach. Similarly, a disregard for the future is a mark of undeveloped men. They take present actions with little regard for posterity, or even for outcomes a decade removed in the future. They live as the primitive, for the present moment. Wyndham Lewis in *Time and Western Man* described this tendency as "time patriotism," or "time

chauvinism," corresponding in spirit to the place patriotism with which we are more familiar. Where one says, "My country, right or wrong," the other says, "My time, right or wrong"; and so the excessive mass egocentricity of a new modernism enters, scorning the past as traditionalism, the future as utopianism, having a blind spot toward eternity, and reserving the historic and prophetic sense for intellectual and spiritual exceptionals.

For all this, there is an unconscious mass time sense running far deeper than the conscious, binding ages together with the social inheritance handed down by written and spoken words, and even more by the patterns of folkways, from generation to generation.

With the growth of the historic sense and its accompanying extension of the area of effective events rose the problem of measurement in groups of years, or cycles. The various means of counting years are far from universal even today, although the calendar of the Christian Era is recognized the world over. It was normal that, at first, the years should be scored off from outstanding events of local or national interest—and nations were simply large localities or tribes. Some notable event in the memory of each particular culture marked its own "beginning," and years were counted from that event until another supplanted it in the public's sense of importance. The Jews dated at first from such occasions as the Passover, the Exile, the building of the Temple, or the reigns of the kings, until the Creation itself was settled upon as the true beginning of time—later, by Marcus Terentius Varro, friend of Pompey and Cicero, given the date corresponding to our 3761 B.C., still traditional with modern Jews. This was revised to 4004 B.C. in the Christian tradition as computed by Archbishop Ussher in the chronology appended to many editions of the King James Bible. The birth of Abraham, 2016 B.C., as a starting point was introduced by Eusebius in the fourth century A.D. and was used for a time.

The Romans dated things from 753 B.C., according to Varro the date of the legendary founding of the city, Romulus having yoked a bullock and a heifer to a plow on April 21 or 24 of that year to break ground for the building. Their years were marked "A.U.C.," meaning *ab urbe condita*—"from the founding of the city." Later the Roman counting was obscured by the conceits of emperors who insisted upon marking time from their own conquests, birthdays, or reigns. This complicated and confused historic studies, often gave a distorted picture, and lingered long into the Christian Era, alongside the Christian datings. Illustrating the awkwardness of this sort of counting is the following ending of a letter from Pope Honorius of Rome to Bishop Honorius in England in A.D. 634, quoted by the Venerable Bede:

Given the eleventh day of June, in the twenty-fourth year of the reign of our most pious emperor, Heraclius, and the twenty-third after his consulship; and in the twenty-third of his son Constantine, and the third after his consulship; and in the third year of the most illustrious Caesar, his son Heraclius, the seventh of our indiction; that is, in the year of the incarnation of our Lord, 634.

The "indiction" was first an imperial and later a papal designation meaning a fifteen-year period beginning January 1, December 25, or March 25. A simple formula to determine the indiction is to add 3 to the year of our Lord and divide by 15. The quotient is the indiction and the remainder is the year of the indiction.

The Greeks, lacking a single decisive historic event, marked their years in "Olympiads," the four-year intervals

between the great games, which began July 1, 776 B.C. For instance, an event would take place in a certain year of a certain Olympiad. Meton, 432 B.C., was the Greek calendarer who introduced nineteen-year cycles.

The Chinese began things 2697 B.C. with the official introduction of sixty-year cycles at that time. Modern Chinese date from the Revolution of 1912, which is celebrated October 10, and also use the Gregorian calendar. The Mohammedans begin time at the Hegira, the flight of the prophet Mohammed from Mecca to Medina, A.D. 622, their years being designated "A.H."—"year of the Hegira." The imperial conceits of old Rome reappeared in our time with Mussolini's attempt to supplant the world-accepted calendar with the date of his march on the city. And Hitler sought to begin a new era commemorating himself and the origin of the Third Reich.

For all these confusions in different cultures the single great event that over all the world divides time in two is the birth of Christ. Of such commanding importance is that event that any different datings must be supplemented with that of the Christian Era, and there is no occasion in all history but must be marked either before or after the birth of our Lord. The confusions we have noted are common to all pre-Christian and non-Jewish calendars for lack of any decisive event great enough to dominate. The Jews, in giving the world the Creation, and the Christians, the Incarnation, thus symbolize in calendar usage the all-commanding position of our common spiritual tradition over all particular secular cultures and competing faiths.

Sub Specie Aeternitatis

In this evolution may also be noted religion's introduction of the sense of eternity into time, with spiritual and political meanings given to long stretches such as millennia, and the scope of things extended backward to the Creation and forward toward the final consummation. The Jews made a division between the "present age" and the "age to come."

The Christians also had a strong sense of coming things and the final consummation. This emphasis in Judaism and Christianity is called "eschatology," or the doctrine of the "end of the present order on earth and the establishment of the reign of eternity."

Scientific development also introduces ever-increasing measurements, requiring such staggering units as the geological "eon," a word descriptive of any of the grand divisions of geological change. Historic studies also indicate the rhythm of social nature on a scale far vaster than sunrises or tides or seasons with the discovery of the great renaissances at intervals of several centuries, which, in the general awakening of life, may indicate historic springtimes, and even point to the possibility of seasonal recurrence on a cosmic scale.

Results of the wider reaches of the new physics and astromathematics upon the spiritual life of man may not now be appraised. The present concern of science with the nature of time, space, and light, those natural phenomena which by their mysteriousness to ordinary men seem suggestive of spirit, arouses also new metaphysical and psychic speculations, many of them fantastic. Yet the suggestion remains that in this marvelous universe there is no exact line of demarcation between the natural and spiritual orders. Astronomy, the oldest of the sciences, holds to ancient mythological nomenclature even to this ultramodern day. While newer branches of learning adopt specialized vocabularies of new technical coinage, the study of the stars still uses the language of the myth, the folk story, or the fairy tale, and fills the sky with bears, queens, lions, and kings. And the language of folkways is close to that of religion.

These vaster stretches of time, however, will have small present bearing upon our interest in this book, as also the divisions smaller than the day. Avoiding the temptation to speculate upon the meanings of either the infinitely small or the infinitely large, we are content to understand our culture, whose generations and centuries are a brief season in the passage of time, and reverently to remember that even the life of our small planet is *sub specie aeternitatis*—under the providence of the sovereign God to whom "a thousand years ... are but as yesterday when it is past." In the newer understanding, time represents the immobile, changeless ground of the universe. The "Fountain of Time" sculpture of Lorado Taft in Washington Park, Chicago, is the symbolic refutation of the old adage that "time flies." For here the majestic robed figure of Time stands still, while in the frieze historic events pass in review before him.

Of more immediate bearing upon religious observances is the thought of the brevity of human memory, which needs periodical arousing to keep men faithful. The psychology of the second generation seems always to dampen original ardor. The vital religious impulse of the fathers is not automatically transmissible to the sons, but requires revival through instructional return to origins. The Jews in exile, but for the unwelcome preachments of the prophets, might have forgotten the faith of the fathers entirely and adopted foreign ways. The writer of the letter to the Hebrews was concerned with this same tendency among the second-generation Christians, who under the blandishments of a different culture and the threat of persecution were forgetting what had made them Christian. In both these cases a liturgical concern helped to preserve the faith until circumstances were more favorable for making it vital again.

Time also reminds us we need perspective on the historical scene. Things must be seen by longer range, and it is this long range of religion that redeems man from his bent to contemporaneity. There are temporal distortions in all our minds, somewhat like the spatial distortions found in old maps. A medieval map of Europe, for instance, presents a somewhat misshapen mass of land as most of the earth. It is surrounded by the desert on the south, a fringe of frozen ocean on the north, dragon-infested seas to the westward, and a mysterious east of fable and riches. So our limited time sense maps our present and bounds it with the crudest ideas of history and the future, resulting in distorted valuations. This led Bede to note that "it often happens that those who are at a distance, sooner than others, understand the things that need correction." In the recurring observations of past persons and events, this process of evaluation matures; we "see things steadily and see them whole."

Time, too, has been religiously presented as a sacred trust, which one is to keep and "redeem." It is as though we were granted a certain portion of this illimitable supply of time, so rich in its possibilities, and charged with its proper keeping. Having only so much to use in the brief course of life, one uses it well who spends it in memory of the dealings of God through history.

The Founding of Calendars

The line between natural and artificial is hard to draw, but somewhere begins the conscious association of events with times and places. What started as the instinctive seasonal movement of the mass, unreasoned and unplanned, takes on the character of a stated observance and becomes embedded in the stream of official tradition. That such seasonal observances are common to all cultures, primitive and advanced, would seem to establish the universality of the habit in human nature itself rather than in the inventiveness of particular cultures or priestly classes. The official institution of a ceremony comes late, and is usually merely the open recognition of a usage already long established by the common practice.

We have seen that passage into agricultural development gives an added impetus to public observances. It is with the early agricultural civilizations that time consciousness first turns into the art and science of calendar making. The Egyptian civilization made the first important contribution, and

one of the chief reasons for this was the fact that Egypt was the world's granary. Here the wide cultural significance of calendar development is seen in religious, scientific, economic, and historical implications. The first work is done by priests, joining scientific curiosity with the desire to regularize religious practices. "The determination of dates for seasonal festivals early made the precision of the calendar important, and naturally placed it in priestly hands, so that this oldest of the sciences has always possessed a sacerdotal or ecclesiastical character." [3]

The scientific interest also developed far along astronomical and meteorological lines, continuous with the Babylonian astrology from as early as 2400 B.C. There was also the practical bearing of calendar making on the planting and gathering of crops. Mathematical and historical interests, both illustrated by the pyramids, obelisks, and monuments, grew along with the advancing time consciousness, the chronologies or reigns and dynasties being commemorated in the planes

---

[3] H. B. Alexander in *Dictionary of Religion and Ethics.*

and solids of a dramatic national geometry. Thus calendar making ramified throughout the social life of early Egypt, where the movement culminated in the complete system of the Ptolemies of Alexandria, almost contemporaneously with the rise of Christianity. This system held until Copernicus, in the fifteenth century after Christ.

The Ptolemaic astronomy, we have said, was the culmination of the traditional system rather than the formulation of a new. Ptolemy drew upon the work of Apollonius and Hipparchus, accepting the long-prevailing idea of an earth-centered system in which time in its longer seasonal and annual stretches was measured by the movements of the moon, the year being from five to twelve months long. This was the device of the whole early world; therefore the chronology of the Bible is that of the lunar rather than the solar year. The sun served its purpose for marking the boundaries of the day; but months, seasons, and the year were determined by the moon. The very earliest years were no doubt quite inexact— a crude designation for "a long time"—and the tendency to exactness was developed later. This understanding of the meaning of the year is of service in many ways in Old Testament interpretation, in such matters, for instance, as the long life span of the patriarchs.

The Jewish calendar is a parallel development to the Egyptian, the astronomy of the latter having been accepted, then Jewish days and seasons being introduced after the Exodus. Practically all the religious items of the Jewish calendar today are definitely traceable to the earliest Old Testament accounts of their history. A thousand years before Christ the Jews had a twelve-month lunar calendar, every item of which was filled with political and religious meaning. Later a thirteenth month was added periodically to take up the accumulated slack between sun year and moon year. The moon's passage around the earth requires 29 days, 12 hours, 44 minutes, and 3 seconds; hence the twelve lunar months total 354 days, 8 hours, 48 minutes, and 36 seconds. This is short of the solar year, as noted above, by 10 days, 21 hours, and 9.51 seconds. The insertion of the thirteenth month every leap year more nearly balances the equation. Modern Jews still use this traditional calendar for religious and cultural observances, together with the prevailing civil calendar.

In Rome, in 46 B.C., Julius Caesar assembled his scholars, borrowed heavily from Egyptian learning, and, through assistance of the philosopher Sosigenes, corrected the work of the Greek Meton. On January 1, 45 B.C., or 708 A.U.C., he introduced to the Roman world the reform known as the Julian calendar. This supplanted the old Roman, which had fallen into confusion through abuse of the pagan pontiffs, whose business it was to create new divinities for all occasions. The Julian calendar set the norm for the civilization of the West for some fifteen centuries. Like our present calendar, it measured the year in 365 days—twelve months—with an extra day once in four years. The relative accuracy of this calendar over the Jewish, Egyptian, and old Roman is seen in the fact that during the fifteen centuries of its use it went out of line only ten days, and is now only thirteen days short of our own.

✳The Christian calendar began with Christian features introduced into the Jewish and Roman schedules. All the first Christians were Jews and, as such, continued the Jewish celebrations with faithfulness. In the New Testament there is no direct reference to any yearly festivals among the later Gentile Christians, though it may be assumed they kept the Passover when they were with Jewish Christians, as the occasion marking the last events of the Lord's life. Sunday was observed from the first as a day of celebration of the resurrection, following the Jewish Sabbath. By the fourth century the main features of the present Christian Year had made their appearance, perhaps in the following order: Easter, Pentecost, Ascension Day, Epiphany, Christmas, completing the basic frame to which other items would be added right down to the present. By the third century a cult of martyrs had been added to the calendar concerns. In A.D. 527 the monk Dionysius Exiguus, called the Little, rebelling against the use of pagan datings, first marked off time by the birth of Christ into "A.C." (*ante Christum*) and "A.D." (*anno Domini*). There is no reason advanced why the Latin "A.D." was continued, while the "A.C." was translated into English, "B.C." ("before Christ"). A more recent usage, frequently found in modern Jewish writers, refers to these periods as "C.E." ("common era") and "B.C.E." ("before the common era"). From early days inaccurate calculation placed the Lord's birth probably four years after the actual event, which error still prevails in our numbering of the years.

There were no further major changes until the Renaissance, when Copernicus, the astronomer of the modern world as Ptolemy was of the ancient, moved the study to a sun-centered basis. While this was revolutionary to astronomy and terrific in its theological results, there was no comparable effect upon the calendar, whose usages were firmly fixed in social habit. Yet the general awakening of the times stimulated Pope Gregory XIII to institute the reform known as the Gregorian calendar, which was called "new style" to distinguish from the "old style," or Julian, and which is the common civil schedule of today the world over. His experts, Christopher Clavius and Aloysius Lilius, corrected the ten days' error which, we have seen, had accumulated under the Julian calendar. The lag was corrected by papal edict, October 5, 1582, becoming October 15. And the future was taken care of by the simple means of omitting leap year when it would fall upon years ending in hundreds, except multiples of four hundred. This is said to have reduced the factor of error to a single day in five thousand years. In the technical treatise *The Christian Calendar and the Gregorian Reform* Peter Archer shows the full astronomical significance of this change.

The slow adoption of the rather simple Gregorian reform is an illustration of how deeply rooted calendars are in the social custom, and how they must grow from the change of experience rather than by superimposition. It was not until 1752, two hundred years later, that the Gregorian calendar was adopted by England and the American colonies. And only in 1923 Russia authorized its adoption to take effect September 30, 1943, which date was followed the next day by October 14, to correct the thirteen-day error which by now has accumulated under the Julian calendar.

During all this time the Christian Ecclesiastical Year as we know it was in process of development, parallel with the growth of civil calendars, borrowing and discarding customs of the prevailing culture modes. Its growth is that of a forest which flourishes by the natural pruning and purging of its dead stock as well as by the sprouting of new, or like a language with its obsolescences and new coinages.

Our present calendars, civil and religious, show strong influences from both Jews and Romans, and the clearer understanding of our present problem calls for brief résumés of these two schemes, the one of the mother faith from which we grew, the other of the hostile culture in opposition to which we emerged.

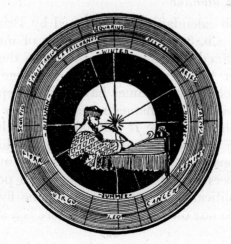

Chapter II

THE JEWISH CEREMONIAL YEAR

THE Old Testament is full of references to the Jewish commemorations. Here we can trace the origin and development of the celebrations still kept in modern Judaism. Help is thus offered on many points of Old Testament interpretation; and, further, knowledge of this cultural background deepens appreciation for the Jewish culture contemporary with our own. For instance, a knowledge of the original identity between the Passover and the Lord's Supper should not only enhance mutual appreciations but also offer the basis for interfaith observances. Instances of this have already occurred. On the cultural level the Jews universally accept Christmas; and there is, correspondingly, a growing recognition of the Jewish New Year on the part of Christians, often with interchange of gifts and felicitations on both occasions.

The Jewish Calendar

The Jewish calendar was sanctioned by Prince Hillel II in Palestine, A.D. 360, after the customs of many centuries had already fixed it in the public usage. In the table below, the names of the months show the Babylonian influence, some of the old Jewish names having been replaced during the Exile, and the new names remaining after the Restoration. The numbers in the *R* column indicate the position of the month in religious usage, Tishre being the first month of the religious year, beginning, as our own, in the autumn.

The numbers in the *P* column show the position of the month in political usage, Nissan being the first, somewhat removed from our own New Year. There is a strong note of

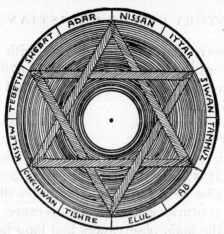

national independence in the change of the New Year as
recorded in Exodus 12:1-2. The Great Deliverance, taking
place in the seventh month of the old religious year, converted the seventh to the first month. A new beginning was
made, which was to secure political independence and national growth to a people formerly slaves; and the Lord
himself recognized the new epoch, commanding: "This month
shall be unto you the beginning of months: it shall be the
first month of the year." The biblical datings thereafter are
on the political scheme. The Jewish calendar follows:

R	P	NAME OF MONTH	NO. OF DAYS	CORRESPONDING TO:
7	1	Nissan	30	March–April
8	2	Iyyar	29	April–May
9	3	Siwan	30	May–June
10	4	Tammuz	29	June–July
11	5	Ab	30	July–August
12	6	Elul	29	August–September
1	7	Tishre	30	September–October
2	8	Chechwan	29–30	October–November
3	9	Kislew	29–30	November–December
4	10	Tebeth	29	December–January
5	11	Shebat	30	January–February
6	12	Adar	29–30	February–March
	13	Vedar	29 (intercalary—leap year only)	

41

We have seen that the Jewish era, with Varro, came to be dated from the Creation, supposedly 3761 B.C. Hence, to find the current year, we simply add that figure to the year of our civil calendar.

The Ceremonies

The Jewish ceremonial traditions are traceable to the earliest days. It is likely that even in Egypt certain practices of the slave tribe were forming. The first written accounts, five or more centuries after the Deliverance, indicate that the forms of the main observances had long been practiced, and had been of primary help in forming the Jewish character and culture throughout the wilderness years and into the period of the development of the kingdom. It is important to note that the first written accounts of ceremonies, those in Deuteronomy, were accomplished only after the decline from the golden age of David, which culminated in invasion and spoliation.

The first Old Testament writings are prophetic. The absorbing interest is in the contemporary world with its social, moral, and political situations. But only after national ruin does the ritualistic tradition find its way into the biblical literature with the writing of Deuteronomy, probably about 693 B.C. The name of this writing, meaning "second law," suggests a former lost book or oral tradition. A half century later this roll was discovered and given circulation in the reform reign of Josiah. It was not until the Persian period, around 350 B.C., that the ceremonial prescriptions were expanded to the Deuteronomy of our present Bible, at which time there appeared also the other books from Genesis to Joshua which are filled with the ceremonial rites of the Jews. This brief account indicates one of the chief uses of observances, that of conserving a culture from ruin or re-establishing it after ruin. It shows also that calendars become official only after long usage has established their practices in the people.

The frame of the Jewish year is composed of the Sabbath and the three chief festivals: the Passover, Pentecost, and the Feast of Tabernacles. All were, no doubt, very ancient ceremonies, antedating even the historic events later associated with them. This frame grew to the present proportions, which will be briefly sketched. These basic items are authorized in Exodus, defined more fully in the Levitical Code, and are frequently referred to elsewhere. The seasonal influence is seen upon each of the three main events. It is possible they were celebrated in the folkways even before the happenings which they later came to commemorate. The Passover, besides recalling the deliverance from bondage, is a natural spring festival; Pentecost, in addition to commemorating the Ten Commandments, is a lesser agricultural festival; and the Feast of Tabernacles, besides celebrating the wilderness years, is a year-end thanksgiving.

Abraham Z. Idelsohn's *The Ceremonies of Judaism* offers in brief compass about what the Protestant Christian would like to know about these historic beginnings, and a knowledge of the rich worship content of the celebrations would add to that Christian's own experience the element of a far greater antiquity. We here offer a condensed account of the main features of the Jewish year, drawing mainly from Idelsohn and the Old Testament sources.

The Sabbath

The Sabbath is the basic institution of the Jewish scheme. An old proverb recognized its high position in saying, "Israel could not exist without the Sabbath." The primitive superstitious regard for the number seven not only accounts for the origin of this important day, said to have come from the Egyptian *sabo,* but is extended later to give a wide and deep social significance to the "week of years," or "prophetic week," followed by the "sabbatical year" and the "seven weeks of years," in turn followed by the year of jubilee,

coming once in fifty. The sabbatical year and the year of
Jubilee were full of social and ethical requirements of an
unusually high order. They served as a check against the
economic process which, if left alone, would end in inequali-
ties. Those in bondage were periodically set free in the
seventh year; and it was a sound principle of soil conserva-
tion, worthy of a much later period, that the land itself had
had rest. The sabbatical year remains with us today in the
system of extending a year's leave of absence, once in seven,
to members of university faculties. And the year of jubilee
is carried over into the celebrations of the fiftieth year of
local churches. A Book of Jubilees appeared in the second
century B.C., offering a Jewish calendar based on a forty-
nine-year cycle. It was part of the anti-Greek reaction.

The origin of the Sabbath Day was traditionally placed
at the Creation, when God himself set the precedent of rest
after the week of labor. Thereafter it is enjoined as a commandment, and the people are admonished to keep it as a
sign. The day which began, as we have seen, in ominous
fear of taboo, to be avoided as unlucky for work, is elevated
to a day of joy, worship, and religious instruction. The
directions at first do not go beyond abstention from labor,
but a little later it is accepted as the proper time for as-
semblage. Beautiful home customs also grew up around
the Sabbath, the time being redeemed from mere idleness
to one of teaching the young the ways of the fathers and of
the Lord's dealings. The rabbis reinterpreted the meaning
of the day from time to time in the light of advancing

spiritual and ethical concep-
tions. Yet the continuing
sternness of the early days
remained, and the first punishment by death for Sab-
bath violation is recorded in
Numbers. A man was dis-
covered gathering sticks, and

was brought before Moses, Aaron, and the assembled people for judgment, there being no precedent as yet; whereupon he was stoned to death.

The importance of the Sabbath greatly increased during the Exile, when forced labor and constant surveillance interfered with the main festivals. But the hardships of the Exile, or the later Greek and Roman persecutions, could not prevail over this precious day. Here was the one time when, in the privacy of their homes, the wanderers could sing the songs of Israel, though in a strange land. There was also a scribal concern that the faith be kept pure in heathen surroundings, so the Sabbath customs were elaborated upon and new rules for its keeping evolved. This tendency to legalize continued into the Restoration and thereafter, finally reaching the absurdity of the Pharisees from which Jesus and Paul revolted.

Preparation for the day began on Friday, continuing until the time of "separation" at the conclusion of Friday evening with the service of Habdalah. This idea of the separation between the sacred and the profane is fundamental to the whole matter of religious celebrations, setting apart from common things the special days, places, books, and persons, and conferring upon them a peculiar sanctity. While the idea, ramifying through religious history, needs the check of its paradox, which sees God's presence everywhere, the sense of separation is still a necessary accompaniment of deep and vital religious experience. Without the paradox it is corrupted into a sort of privileged specialization. But without the idea of separation, the sense of God's presence everywhere becomes vaguely pantheistic. The Jews in their Sabbath were putting to use this principle of separation which at its best seeks to make religion real by making it different from the common life.

I shall pass over the history of how the Jewish calendar developed, and offer a summary of the main features as they are observed throughout Jewry today.

The New Year

The Jewish New Year, Rosh Hashana, is celebrated as chief of the high holidays on the first day of Tishre, the first month of the religious year. It falls in September or October of our calendar, and has something of the same spirit as our civil New Year's Day. The rabbis have given a varying content of meaning to the celebration, including the "day of memorial" of God's dealings, and the "day of judgment" over evil. There is an emphasis upon the worth of the individual regardless of nationality, and on the corresponding value of human universality. A hundred blasts of the shophar drive the evil spirits away and recall the providence of God. The shophar is the ram's horn of the Abraham and Isaac story. This commemoration is described in Leviticus as the Feast of Trumpets, with instructions to observe it as a day of rest, convocation, and offering. And in Numbers, further details are given as to the making of the instruments of silver, an improvement upon the original ram's horn, to be used not only for the high days but for the camp bugle calls. Conventional greetings between Jews on this day are: "May you be inscribed for a good year"; "May it be His will that this year be a sweet one"; and "May God cast our sins into the depths of the seas."

Ten days of penitence are observed from Rosh Hashana to Yom Kippur. Within this period, on the third day of Tishre, the Fast of Gedaliah memorializes the governor of Palestine of that name, whose death on the day after Rosh Hashana, 586 B.C., marked the destruction of Jewish independence.

46

The Day of Atonement

The Day of Atonement, or Yom Kippur, concluding the ten penitential days, is on the tenth day of Tishre. The account of its founding is in Leviticus 23:26-32. Ethically and religiously crude in its origin, it has come to be retranslated into a day of penitence, forgiveness, and charity. Preparation for the day consisted of sending a scapegoat into the desert bearing away the sins of the people, a somewhat irresponsible notion of reconciliation with God. Ancient customs of sacrifices of fowls and coins still survive, although opposed by modern rabbis, with whom charity supplants the ancient blood offerings. Yom Kippur is a sacred time of prayer and meditation, such as our Good-Friday; and as the culmination of the New Year's preparation, the day elevates the

teaching that we are reconciled to God only as we seek reconciliation with our neighbors.

The Feast of Tabernacles

The Feast of Tabernacles (or Booths), called Succoth, begins four days after Yom Kippur and extends through the week from the fifteenth to the twenty-second day of Tishre. It also is described in Exodus as the feast of the year end, or late harvest, and is referred to in Josephus. The occasion now commemorates the life of Israel in the desert. This is the Jewish Thanksgiving, very like our own in its remembrance of the wilderness days of the Pilgrim Fathers and in the harvest festival significance. Booths are erected, symbolic of simplicity, frailty, and humility, the custom originating after the destruction of the Temple; and the devout Jew is to live the whole week in his booth, engaging in prescribed celebration. The feeling of the occasion is expressed in its designation as the "Feast of Our Rejoicing"; in the prayer "I beseech Thee O Lord, grant us salvation; I beseech Thee O Lord, grant us prosperity"; and in the announcement "A Voice proclaims good tidings."

On the day following Succoth, which is the twenty-third of Tishre, Rejoicing of the Law, or Simchath Torah, is observed. Corresponding somewhat to our Universal Bible Sunday, it is the day in which the Jew rejoices in his posses-

sion of the holy law, singing, "Be strong and fortified in your championing of the Torah."

The Feast of Lights

The Feast of Lights, or the Feast of Dedication, called Chanukah, is kept on the twenty-fifth day of Kislew, or Ethanim of the older usage. It emphasizes the victory of the Maccabees over Antiochus Epiphanes, who had ordered a pagan altar set up at Jerusalem in 165 B.C., and the restoration of the Temple in 162 B.C. These events were supposed to have been foretold in the prophecies of Daniel. This is one of the later additions to the Jewish calendar, said to

have been decreed by Judas Maccabaeus himself. The historian Josephus gives an account of the celebration, connecting it with the ancient prophecy. In its two meanings it recalls the foundation as well as the purification of the Temple, with the theme of the conquest of darkness by light. The eight-branch candelabrum is its central symbol. Handel has celebrated this occasion in the aria "The Feast of Lights" in his *Judas Maccabaeus*. This ancient day has an influence upon our own dedication ceremonies, usually observed upon completion of a church building, and in some cases upon its being paid for in full. Since Protestantism has no central temple, some local churches celebrate their anniversaries as annual dedication days, giving them more special emphasis upon the even decades, particularly the fiftieth, or the year of Jubilee.

Six weeks after Chanukah, on the fifteenth day of Shebat, Chamishah Asar Bishvat is observed as a sort of minor Arbor Day, honoring the native fruits of Palestine, mainly the carob, or St. John's bread. This seedlike nut is thought to have been "the husks that the swine did eat," of the prodigal son story. It also grows in California.

Another minor occasion is the Fast of Tebeth, on the tenth day of that month, which was probably of seasonal significance.

The Feast of Lots

The Feast of Lots, or Purim, is the most dramatic of the celebrations. It falls on the fourteenth day of Adar (or on the second of Adar in leap years) and is a joyous and somewhat noisy dramatization of the entire book of Esther, celebrating the escape of the Jews from Ahasuerus the Persian. This is the latest feast to be added to the Jewish Year, the

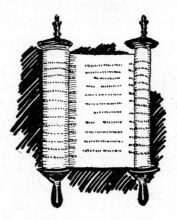

book of Esther having been written about 150 B.C. to explain the origin of the feast, which it seeks to push back to the fifth century B.C. It is an outstanding illustration of how a celebration may be established by superimposition rather than by social growth. It is a gala occasion with many customs similar to our Christmas customs, including exchange of gifts and the use of decorations, cakes, noisemakers, and other holiday appurtenances. At the convocation the text of the Esther scroll is read with dramatic accompaniments. Haman the villain is burned in effigy, and at each mention of his name in the reading of the scrip the whirr of the noisemakers serves as hissing. The day has become a chief symbol of the Jews, marking their release from sufferings, persecutions, and villifications and being something of a compensation for the unjust position they have held in society. The poor are remembered on this day, as well as friends and

18330

relatives; and the home circle is brightened with banqueting and joy. The customs of the day advanced the drama with the stimulus to the production of Purim plays, and music and painting were furthered by the tradition.

The Passover

The Passover, or Pesach, from the fifteenth to the twenty-first of Nissan, is the Jewish celebration most familiar to

Christians because of its close connection with New Testament events. It is instituted as one of the three major feasts in Exodus, in commemoration of Israel's liberation from the "four hundred and thirty years" of Egyptian bondage, through the intervention of the angel of death who, while killing the Egyptian first-born, "passed over" the houses of the Jews, designated for the purpose on the preceding evening by lamb's blood smeared on the lintels. It refers also to the "passage over" the Red Sea. It is likely that the institution is rooted in some traditional folk custom which was utilized in the escape. There are many traditions associated with it traceable to the Arab Bedouins and other Eastern peoples. The Passover is kept as the Feast of Unleavened Bread, recalling the haste with which the people left Egypt, carrying with them the yet unleavened dough prepared on the previous evening. As this unleavened bread was the chief food in the first desert days, it is the chief article of the table during the whole week of the observance. A faithful Jew

51

Pearlman Memorial Library
Central Bible Institute
Springfield, Missouri

will not be without the matzi during the Passover, even though he must be supplied through the charity of his friends. The slaughtering of the lamb according to traditional directions is also part of the preparation. In the time of Cestius in Palestine 256,500 lambs were estimated as the Passover supply. This is one of the indexes for calculating population, a lamb supposedly supplying ten people.

The event has also a seasonal significance, being in the spring of the year and Judaism having incorporated the natural spring festivities into their custom, as Christians later incorporated them into Easter. In Leviticus the "wave offering" is added to the celebrations, being a symbolic enactment of the sprinkling of blood upon the lintels. The theme of the period is national and personal liberty.

A second Passover is authorized in Numbers, one month from the first, for the accommodation of those who because of defilement from handling dead bodies were unfit for participation in the first.

This great celebration appears many times in the Old Testament. It is a rally occasion for Joshua's forces at Gilgal before Jericho in preparation for the siege; and great leaders like Josiah use it as a means of the reconsecration of the people after idolatry.

The service of Seder, held in the home, precedes Passover.

Haggadah is the home version of the Passover ritual which came into use in the family circle after the destruction of the Temple. This service is still widely used by the Jewish people to supplement their public convocation.

One is impressed with the rather intense Jewishness of the earliest accounts of the Passover, later modified in the direction of hospitality. The first orders are negatively stated, to the effect that *no stranger* may partake of the Passover without having received circumcision. In later accounts, the tone is changed to a more positive note, the effect being that the stranger within the gates *may* partake provided he has met the ritualistic requirement.

The Sefirah Lag Boamer follows, a forty-nine-day penitential period similar to our Lent. Marriages may not be performed in this season, haircutting is postponed, and eggs are part of the mourning food. This commemorates a racial crucifixion of A.D. 135, when a million Jews were killed in reprisal for the uprising led by Bar Cocheba against the Roman rule.

Pentecost

Pentecost, or the Feast of Weeks, called Shabuoth, marks the close of the post-Passover season on the sixth day of Siwan. This is seven weeks, or fifty days, after the Passover; and the name "Pentecost" shows the influence of the Greek period. It celebrates the thanksgiving at the first harvest, as

described in Exodus and Numbers, and also the giving of the Ten Commandments to Israel, and later the Torah. Reformed Judaism revived it as confirmation date, remembering that Israel was confirmed in the faith by Moses. It was on this day that the early Christians experienced the visitation of the Holy Spirit which marked the birthday of the Christian Church. They were, no doubt, participating in the celebrations at the time, when Peter used the occasion for delivering a powerful sermon in which the whole history of the Jews was traced to its promised fulfillment in the Christ. His winning of three thousand converts launched the Church upon its historic mission.

The Fast of Tammuz, or the Three Weeks' Tish'a Be'ab, begins on the seventeenth day of Tammuz and ends on the ninth of Ab. During these weeks the Jews mourn for the two destructions of their Temple, once at the time of the devastation by Nebuchadnezzar, 586 B.C., and again at the Dispersion by Titus, A.D. 70. Renunciations and lamentations characterize the occasion, which comes to its close with the Fast of Ab, on the ninth day of that month.

Prophets and Psalmists

During the whole development of ritual through the Old Testament, warnings against formalism are raised by the prophets and psalmists. A tense polarity exists between the inwardness and outwardness of religion, or between its formal symbolic expressions and its ethical and spiritual requirements. While the prophets wrote before the liturgists, we discover the long existence of rites and ceremonies in the fact that these prophetic spirits inveigh against the idolatrous abuses of religious rites. Micah represents this continuing criticism of formalism in his famous controversy between the Lord and the people: "Wherewith shall I come before the Lord, and bow myself before the high God? shall I come before him with burnt offerings, with calves of a year old? Will the Lord be pleased with thousands of rams, or with ten thousands of rivers of oil? shall I give my first-born for my transgression, the fruit of my body for the sin of my soul?" And his answer to the moral decay of dead ritualism is in that "diamondlike utterance of the sum total of human duty," sometimes called the Golden Rule of the Old Testament: "He hath shewed thee, O man, what is good; and what doth the Lord require of thee, but to do justly, and to love mercy, and to walk humbly with thy God."

The psalms, too, sing that strain, notably the fiftieth, which minimizes the importance of ceremonies and challenges the idea of separation between sacred and secular. The animals of the sacrifice are nothing to God: "For every beast of the forest is mine, and the cattle upon a thousand hills."

Yet we may well think that the deep meanings within the rich cultural practices of their people were dear to the hearts of psalmists and prophets, and that their burden was not against these things but rather against their idolatrous abuse. The Psalms, in fact, were the hymnbook; and the chief use of these marvelous songs, running the whole gamut of human experiences, was in the celebrations and the regular convocations. Many of the great antiphonies presuppose an intricate pattern of liturgy, as do those that celebrate the use of musical instruments to the glory of God. They were used on such special occasions as the moving of the ark, and for such purposes as exhortation to keep the law and rehearse the covenant. They urge the people to faithful observation of the ordinances of remembrance, "with a multitude that kept holy day." In exile they voice the longing for the sanctuary and mourn its desolation, with "weeping by the waters of Babylon," keeping the faith pure against the day of retribution.

Chapter III

THE CELEBRATIONS OF PAGAN ROME

B EFORE tracing the development of the Christian festivals in greater detail, I shall show briefly what the Roman Year presented the early community of Christian believers. Both Jewish and Roman calendars are in the background of Christian development—the one, as we have seen, that of the mother faith, the other that of the heathendom from which Christianity reacted. There were departures, of course, from the Jewish, as there were borrowings from the pagan; but the Christian Church Year is to be seen as mainly in continuity with the former and discontinuity with the latter. James Freeman Clarke's *Ten Great Religions* presents the schedule of Roman holidays which forms the basis of the present account. Here and there I shall expand upon the separate items for the sake of giving an impression of the general spirit of Roman celebrations, yet making no effort to tell a complete story.

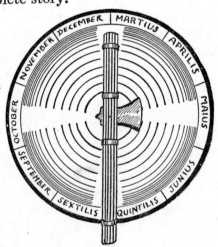

The Roman Calendar

The original Roman year, called the Martial, and traditionally attributed to Romulus, consisted of ten months, totaling 304 days. They were:

OLD ROMAN	NO. OF DAYS	CORRESPONDING TO:
Martius	31	March
Aprilis	30	April
Maius	31	May
Junius	30	June
Quintilis	31	July
Sextilis	30	August
September	30	September
October	31	October
November	30	November
December	30	December

Reckoning of years was later adopted, by Varro, from 753 B.C., the supposed date of the founding of the city. (The Roman calculations were inaccurate. The Greek, Polybius, set the date 750 B.C. Sir Isaac Newton placed it 627 B.C.)

The close relationship between this calendar and our own is immediately seen. The last four months are still named precisely as they were for several centuries before Christ, and the last six are named simply with their numbers. In four others the translation is direct. And our July and August show the later changes sometimes said to have been ordered by imperial conceit. Numa Pompilius, the second king and successor to Romulus, was probably the true founder of this calendar which has been attributed to Romulus. He later added Januarius and Februarius at the year's end, bringing the year to 355 days, and added an intercalary month, Mercedonius, every second year to equalize. Later, Januarius was placed at the year's beginning. Thus Janus, god of opening and shutting, came to rule over the "gateway month." He also was the god of the whole year, whom Ovid quoted as saying, "All depends on the beginning" —a more prudent observation, perhaps, than "All's well that ends well." From the name "Janus" comes our word "janitor," one who opens and shuts. Februarius was made the second month in 452 B.C. In general use, however, March was continued as the first month until the Gregorian reform, when New Year was established as January 1 to make Septuagesima Sunday fall in the year with its following Easter.

The Roman reckoning of the days of the month was by counting backward from the calends, the first day. The word means "callings," and refers to the callings of the new month by the pontifices after observation of the new moon. Its use remained after calculation took the place of observation, and our word "calendar" is derived from it. The ides fell on the fifteenth day of March, May, July, and October, and the thirteenth in other months. And the nones fell eight days before the ides. This scheme has two interests for us: first, in showing that the Romans knew nothing of the week, using rather the nundinae, or eight-day period between market days. The other is in such literary references as Shakespeare's "The ides of March are come," in *Julius Caesar*.

The temple symbolized both the seasons and the months— the seasons in its four walls; the months in the windows, three to each wall.

The Julian reform was brought about because of abuses of the old calendar by the pagan college of pontiffs, whose power it was to create new gods and assign them days, and by such rulers as added days or even months at their pleasure. While the priestly power over the calendar was ended in 304 B.C., by Gnaeus Flavius, the errors and abuses remained. So the Julian calendar was introduced January 1, 45 B.C., to stabilize the reckoning. This was a 365-day year, with leap year once in four. The intercalary month was dropped. This is the calendar which is now meant by the term "old style," by which it was referred to after the Gregorian reform. In English literature as late as the seventeenth century, for example in George Fox's *Journal,* March is still called the first month.

Augustus restored, rather than reformed, the Julian card, which, by his time had again suffered the extravagances of the rulers, and, according to Suetonius, "had fallen into confusion through negligence." There is a doubtful tradition that Augustus took the occasion to have himself perpetuated in changing the month Sextilis to August, choosing this month rather than September, his birth month, because "in the former he had won his first consulship and most brilliant victories." Whether by the emperor or another, the change was made, an extra day being added to August to make it of equal length with the longest. There were other efforts to rename months for emperors, but none were successful after the time of Augustus.

This was the time scheme at the beginning of Christianity. It is to be expected that the obscure faith would, for some time, have no established calendar of its own, but would rather adopt the computations of the civil order, its own activities being somewhat influenced by pagan customs even while its whole spirit was in competition with the pagan.

The Pagan Celebrations

The Roman year was filled with holidays and celebrations, many going back to Numa Pompilius, the second king, to whom the main religious institutions and traditions of ancient Rome are traced. By the beginning of the Christian Era the whole life of Rome—civil, military, social, and religious—was reflected in these celebrations, which were informed with the spirit of violence, license, and triviality of the period of brilliant decay. Ovid wrote a poetic description of the festivals of the first half year, as they were in vogue after the Julian reform. The accompanying abbreviated catalogue, based upon Clarke, is enough to picture the excesses of the social order in which early Christianity had to make its laborious and suffering way.

Rome showed no creative religious genius but rather borrowed her gods from Greece and other cultures, adapting them to practical, prosaic tasks. They were "working gods," each assigned to duty to the state. While there were often pure and lofty intentions in evidence at the beginning of most of the events, they were all in service to patriotism rather than to religion, and, without exception, they suffered corruption. In fact, there is always a tendency in religious celebrations first toward secularization, then corruption.

The Roman religion was entirely without a doctrinal system; it was altogether ceremonial. As the times degenerated, the ceremonies became spectacles of slaughter of men and animals, orgies of license and drunkenness. Since the Romans worshiped only state-created gods, the gods could be adapted to such uses as seemed good to the state. "There was no limit," wrote Hartung, "to the superficial levity with which the Romans changed their worship." New gods were imported or created on demand, until every commonplace function, every state of mind, and every vice and virtue had its separate god. Deities made by man's devising are subject to man's whims. They are powerless to redeem man; on the other hand, they soon come to personify human nature in its baser aspects. The riotous celebrations of Rome gave our language the term "Roman holiday," applicable to any enjoyment or profit at the expense or suffering of another.

The main features of the Roman year at the time of Christian beginnings are here listed:

JANUARIUS

Added to the original ten-month year by Numa, as the eleventh month; later made first month. Dedicated to Janus, god of opening and shutting.

1   Feast of Janus, celebrating the god of beginnings and protector of peace, with masquerades and excesses

9   Agonalia

11   Carmentalis, honoring the nymph Carmenta. A woman's festival

16   Dedication of the Temple of Concord

31   Feast of the Penates, honoring the household gods

FEBRUARIUS

Added to the original ten-month year by Numa, as the twelfth month; made second month in 452 B.C. Dedicated to Februus, god of purification.

1   Feast of Juno Sospita, honoring the Savior, an old goddess

13–21 Parentalia, chief annual festival of the dead

   13 Faunalia, dedicated to Faunus and the rural gods

   15 Lupercalia, a feast of fruitfulness, also honoring Faunus, whose priests made a circuit of Palatine Hill clad in goatskins, striking all women in their path with thongs, to insure fertility and easy delivery

The abode of Faunus was the Lupercal, referred to in Shakespeare's *Julius Caesar,* in the speech of Anthony:

You all did see that on the Lupercal
I thrice presented him a kingly crown,
Which he did thrice refuse.

This festival is a type of many which exploit the sexual, oftentimes with orgies.

17   Fornacalia, a feast honoring the oven goddess, Fornax

21   Feralia, closing day of Parentalia season, with games

18–28 The Februatio, a feast of purification and atonement

     Februus was an old Etrurian god of the underworld. Also in this period came the Charistia, a family festival for putting an end to quarrels among relations.

23   Feast of Terminus, honoring the god of boundaries, when boundary stones were anointed and crowned—the old year end

MARTIUS

The old first month, so continuing in popular usage until the seventeenth century. Dedicated to Mars, god of war.

1 The Old New Year, and the Feast of Mars, honoring the god of war, when the Salii, priests of Mars go their rounds singing hymns

The Matronalia was added later to make a women's Saturnalia (see December 17). This was also referred to as Juno's Day, Mother of Days, and popularly as Women's Calends, the matrons serving their female servants as at Saturnalia the men serve their slaves. All women received presents from their husbands and friends. The original purpose, to recognize the essential equality of the sexes, was corrupted, and the ruling motif became wantonness.

6 Feast of Vesta
7 Feast of Vejpvis, or Vedius, honoring the boy Jupiter
14 Equira, horse races honoring Mars
15 Feast of Anna Perenna, celebrating the goddess of health
17 Liberalia, Feast of Bacchus, when young men were invested with the Toga Virilis

The corruption of this feast gave our language the term "bacchanalian," signifying "drunken."

19–23 Feast of Minerva, when mechanics, artists, and scholars made offerings honoring intellect

APRILIS

"Opening" month, from the Latin *aperire*.

1 Feast of Venus, in honor of the goddess to whom the month is sacred
4–10 Megalesia, Feast of Cybele and Altys, borrowed from the feasts of Ceres in Greece and Isis in Egypt, with legendary accounts of the origins of the seasons
12 Cerealis, Feast of Ceres, with games in the Circus

15 Fordicidia, Feast of Cows
21 Palilia, Feast of Pales, and of the founding of Rome
23 Vinalia, Feast of New Wine
25 Robigalia, a feast honoring the goddess of blight, Robigo
28 Floralia, a feast honoring the goddess Flora—very licentious

MAIUS

Dedicated to Maia, mother of Hercules.

1 Feast of the Bona Dea, honoring the good goddess Earth

This was the feast held by women secretly in the house of the pontiff, with all males banished.

9 Lemuralia, a feast honoring the departed spirits
12 Games honoring Mars
23 Tubilustria, to consecrate wind instruments

JUNIUS

Dedicated to Juno; also to youth, *junioribus.*

1 Feast of Carna, honoring the goddess of the internal organs of the body, and of Juno Moneta
4 Feast of Bellona
5 Feast of Deus Fidius
7–15 Feast of Vesta
19 Matralia, Feast of Mater Matuta
Other lesser festivals

QUINTILIS–JULIUS

Originally the fifth month, later changed to honor Julius Caesar, who was born on the fourth of its ides.

1 Day devoted to changing residences, like May 1 and October 1 in American cities
4 Fortuna Muliebris
5 Populifuga, in memory of the people's flight on some occasion whose reason was afterward forgotten
7 Feast of Juno Caprotina
15 Feast of Castor and Pollux
Other lesser festivals

63

SEXTILIS–AUGUSTUS

Originally the sixth month, later changed to honor Caesar Augustus.

1   Games in honor of Mars
17   Feast of the god Portumnus
18   Consualia, Feast of Consus, commemorating the rape of the Sabines
23   Vulcanalia, the original fire-prevention day
25   Opeconsivia, Feast of Ops Consiva

SEPTEMBER

The old seventh month. The chief events of this month were the games honoring Juno and Minerva.

OCTOBER

The old eighth month

13   Fontalia, Feast of Fountains, when the springs were strewn with flowers
15   Sacrifice of a horse to Mars

NOVEMBER

The old ninth month. Its feasts are unimportant.

DECEMBER

The old tenth month.

5   Faunalia, in honor of Faunus

17–24 Saturnalia, Festival of Saturn, honoring the god of sowing, whose temple at Rome was founded 497 B.C.

He is identified with the Greek Cronus. The rites were celebrated on the beginning day with a carnival in which the masters served their slaves, in memory of the age of Saturn, when all men were equal. A king was chosen by lot to preside over the festivities. Feasting and exchange of gifts were customs, with the rich keeping open table to all comers, themselves serving the slaves. Schools were closed, and the Senate did not sit. This time of gaiety was early corrupted into a revel of vice, crime, and riot.

Selden refers to it: "Christmas succeeds the Saturnalia, the same time, the same number of days; then the master waited upon the servant, like the lord of misrule."

25   Juvenalis, added to the season by Caligula to make his own permanent addition to gaiety

> During the period, on December 23, offerings were made to the dead at Laurentia's shrine. Laurentia was the nurse of Romulus and Remus.
>
> Juvenalis was the festival of the winter solstice, erroneously calculated December 25 in the Julian calendar.

Quarterly, at each season's beginning, the Feast of Compitalia was observed, when the gods of the crossroads and junctions of the fields were crowned with the season's flowers. These gods were the Lares, who had also household and ancestral functions, and who, together with the Penates, represented the domestic religion of the Roman.

Memorial days for national leaders were popular, and triumphal entries were sought by most of the Caesars, sometimes their prospective enjoyment being the chief motive for waging a war.

The secular games were part of the Roman youth program, physically wholesome in the main, and sometimes, under certain emperors, even stoical in the separation of the sexes, but always with the ruling motive of fitting the youths for soldiery and maidens for bearing sons for the state. The Roman poet Horace is a source of information on these games.

The auguries of public health were similarly wholesome, though directed to fitting the private citizen into the general regimentation for conquest. The superstition of Rome is also seen in the institution of the fifteen grave and learned augurs who observed the face of the heavens or the flight of birds for direction of public affairs.

The pagan excesses are seen in the frequent shows staged by the emperors. Each vied with those preceding in extravagant splendor and ostentatious cruelty. They included pantomime performances, theatrical presentations, extravaganzas, races, athletic contests, and—especially to the liking of the depraved masses—the combats between  gladiators. In these, huge expenditures were made from the public purse; often vast buildings were erected or artificial lakes dug for the occasion, and hundreds of thousands of gladiators lost their lives for the amusement of the spectators. Besides the professional fighters, often citizens and sometimes senators engaged in these contests. Forty thousand men, in Claudius' time, were pitted against each other in a gigantic sea engagement on a constructed lake. They hacked at one another until only one man was left and the sea was filled with blood. On Caligula's succession one hundred sixty thousand victims lost their lives. At least one emperor, Commodus, followed pugilism, winning 1,031 battles before being strangled. Nero, less courageous, performed as a singer at his own games, consistently using his power as emperor to force the judges to award the prize to him.

Centuries later Telemachus, Christian monk, journeyed from Asia to Rome, self-assigned to martyrdom in the cause of abolition of the combats. He rushed into the arena, cried his protest, and was crushed beneath the heels of the contestants. This was Christianity's challenge to this barbarism of the pagan order even more debasing than its military conquests.

The Christian's struggle against this culture and his effort to convert it is a long story, including ten major persecutions that swept the Empire throughout all its provinces, from Palestine to Britain, as the increasing religious effectiveness of the rising cult provoked the fear and wrath of the ruling powers. We shall see how, during this time, Christian observances were established in conscious competition with the orgies of the spring and winter festivals, and how they symbolized in festive occasions the deep opposition between the passing pagan and the rising Christian ways of life.

Historic Christian events take place, worthy to be remembered, and so are incorporated into the ongoing scheme. Every important fact, event, and person becomes included in the archives of communal memory. The biographical interest is conserved through the progressive addition of saints' days, celebrating the conversions and martyrdoms of the great biblical personalities and the fathers and saints coming later. The theological interests are served through days devoted to special doctrines central to Christian faith. Oftentimes major changes of the total plan are accelerated through alterations of established civil calendars and by the revolutionary or reactionary character of changing political regimes or religious epochs. Fasting and feasting, the individual Christian works out his salvation, aided by the reiterations of the Christian Year.

We shall see the story of that development from its earliest beginnings.

Chapter IV

NEW TESTAMENT BEGINNINGS

R ISING and spreading from the dual Jewish-Roman background, the Christian Year adapts and modifies both
these cultural heritages, sometimes content to infuse a
Christian meaning into an old tradition and at other times
sharply breaking in with new revelations, too splendid to be
contained in the old forms. The fulfillment of Judaism and
the conquest of paganism in Christ is dramatized in the
pageantry of the Christian Year, and the pageantry itself
becomes a chief means for propagating the new faith.

As the story continues, these actions and reactions take
place not against outside cultures, but within the Christian
frame itself, continuing modifications with new insights.
Every great controversy within the fellowship leaves its
deposit in the practice of public celebrations. The basic idea
of a formal calendar is never successfully challenged, though
the content is often radically changed. Even in the strongest
antiliturgical movements there is always the expressional
framework of the new experience.

Origin of the Christian Year

The historic origin of the Christian Year may be placed
at the celebration of the Lord's Supper in the weekly meetings of Christians "upon the first day of the week," following their participation in the regular Jewish Sabbath worship. The early followers of Christ were "called Christians
first in Antioch." Until then they considered themselves,
and were considered by the Jews, as a society within the
synagogue. As such, they continued the Jewish ceremonies
with faithfulness. Jesus himself habitually went to the syna-

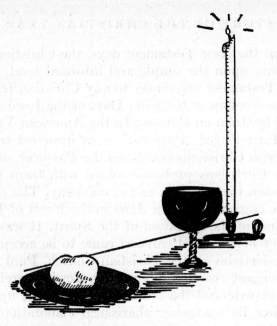

gogue on the Sabbath Day, and on proper occasions he observed the stated festivities of his people.

Passover to Eucharist

The celebration of the Feast of the Passover on the occasion of the Last Supper, with his disciples, is one illustration of his reverential treatment of the ancient customs. While the first Christians put a new spirit into the old rites, some time went on before their own rites became distinctive, with the introduction of their peculiar sacrament and establishment of their Holy Day. The Lord's Supper, though continuous in time with the Feast of the Passover, breaks from it to create something new, in its declaration of forgiveness through the crucified and risen Saviour. More than a mere continuance of an ancient cultural form, the Eucharist is something distinctly new. Similarly, while the Christian's Holy Day has historic association with the Jewish Sabbath, its content is entirely different. That difference, of which the sacrament is the essential part, may be taken as the origin of the Christian Year.

Throughout the New Testament days, the Christian celebrations remain upon the simple and informal level. There are no New Testament references to any Christian festivals other than the worship of the First Day, or the Lord's Day, as it is called by John on Patmos. In the American Version, the use of "Easter" for "Passover" is an incorrect translation. The Jewish Christians continued the Passover, and the later Gentile Christians probably joined with them in this celebration when they were in mixed company. The earliest disciples were engaged with the Jews in the Feast of Pentecost at the time of the visitation of the Spirit. It was more than a century before the Pentecost came to be accepted as distinctly the birthday of the Christian Church. Paul represents the strongest reaction against the Jewish ceremonial law, having experienced the frustration attendant upon an effort to follow its confusing pharisaical elaborations.

Sabbath to Sunday

Because of their close connection in time, the Jewish Sabbath and the Christian Lord's Day have often been confused. It is important to understand their difference. We have seen the essential meaning of the Sabbath in abstention from labor, the only meaning given to it at the time of its institution. It later came to offer an occasion for public convocation, for worship and instruction, and was used as a religious day in the Jewish homelife. The Christian Sunday originally had nothing to do with abstention from labor. It was marked with the custom of breaking bread together "in remembrance of" Him, as the Jewish Christians remained after the Sabbath service into the early hour of the first day of the week. Afterwards they went about their work. To the convenience of the time to the Sabbath was added the significance that it was on this day that the Lord was risen and on this day that the expectant disciples looked for his second coming. So the distinctiveness of the Christian's day is in the sacrament central to all future forms of Christianity and in the joyous celebration of the resurrection and hope of the ultimate consummation. According to Vernon Staley, to whose *The Liturgical Year* we owe most of the following paragraphs, "Sunday, or the Lord's Day, is the most ancient of all the festivals of the Christian Year, being observed from the very first days of Christianity. It is the weekly commemoration of the Resurrection of our Lord." Being from the first a "weekly Easter," this holy day is incorrectly referred to as the "Sabbath," both from the historical standpoint and from that of its spiritual meaning. One need not minimize either the social utility or the disciplinary value of the old Sabbath in remembering this difference.

Significant events occurred on the Lord's Day. It was on this day that Christ appeared five times to the disciples, and after an interval of a week appeared again. The Pentecost of Christian significance fell on Sunday. Paul at Troas met those who come together "upon the first day of the week, . . . to break bread"; and at Corinth he instructed the disciples, "Upon the first day of the week let each one of you lay by him in store, as he may prosper." The last mention of the day is by John, who on the Isle of Patmos "was in the Spirit on the Lord's day." Afterward the evidence pours in from all sides that Sunday was the main Christian Day for prayer, teaching, and the Lord's Supper. The present branches of Christianity which serve communion each Sunday have tradition and spiritual meaning on their side. Sunday without the Eucharist in the early Church was described as "Sunday without the sun." The joy of the occasion is expressed in Cyprian's sentence, "We celebrate the resurrection of the Lord in the morning," and in the Epistle of Barnabas, "We keep the eighth day for rejoicing, in which also Jesus rose from the dead," and again in the teaching of the apostles, "On the Lord's own day gather yourselves together and break bread, and give thanks." In token of that joy, prayer on this day was offered standing, whereas kneeling was the mode on common days.

A beautiful expression of the spirit of fellowship was in the custom of sending the elements of Holy Communion to those absent, as mentioned in Justin Martyr's *Apology*. Alms were also collected on this day. Meanings grow with experience, and the day which originally marked the Lord's resurrection came to mean also the hope of his second coming, and later still was added the thought that "our life also rose through him."

It is readily seen that this beginning of a Christian ceremonial was a fulfillment of the mother faith. The Lord's Supper grew out of the Passover; "as the angel of the Lord had brought life, the Lord himself brought life eternal." And the Christian Sunday emerged from the ancient Sabbath; as God on the seventh day rested from his labor of creation, so on the first day he worked the new creation of man's redemption through the resurrection of his Son. Hooker expressed it thus: "That as one did continually bring to mind the former world finished by creation, so the other might keep us in perpetual remembrance of a far better world begun by him which came to restore all things, to make both heaven and earth new."

It was not until A.D. 200 that the prohibitive note of the fourth commandment was incorporated into the Christian Sunday, with Tertullian's order to abstain from labor; and only with Constantine, A.D. 321, who calls it the "venerable Day of the Sun," was Sunday officially established. The courts and military exercises were then forbidden, though the public games continued. The Council of Laodicea in A.D. 363 introduced compulsory worship and made Sunday labor a crime. In a yet more stringent enactment of A.D. 425, the games, too, were abolished. By the time of Charlemagne there was a general legal establishment of Sunday everywhere. The Sabbath continued for some time in the Eastern Church; but in the West, as Jewish opposition rose, it was converted into a fast day in preparation for the Sunday worship. The last as well as the first of the Christian festivals, this "weekly Easter" survived the periods of antiliturgical bias in subsequent centuries, remaining as the one day recognized even by those branches of Christianity which threw all other elements of ceremony into discard.

As the calendar of Christian observances grew from these beginnings, a Christian theory of forms and symbols grew also. That theory may well be indicated here, to show how the Church valued the proper use of forms while at the same time warning against mere formalism.

Principles of Form

Even the most excessive reactions against accepted outward forms of worship rise from a sound instinct. Two things are necessary to observe in a true evaluation, first, that the inward experience must have some form of outward expression, and, second, that the outward form must be kept in subordination to the inward experience. Genuine faith cannot be too watchful against the tendency in all worship to supplant the spiritual reality with the symbol. Whenever this happens, idolatry has overcome piety. Sacramentalism not only teaches that the reality is communicated by the sign, but also makes a special point of saying that the sign is not the reality—that beyond all things seen, and all particular times and places, are the things not seen which are eternal.

When genuine worship gives way to idolatry, every sort of immoral consequence may be expected to follow. The corruption of devotion by the substitution of false objects for true inevitably results in moral stultification, as the idolaters continue to tithe "mint and anise and cummin" and to observe with nicety all the minutiae of fasting and feasting while forgetting the weightier matters of righteousness and ethical concern. It was against this that the prophets proclaimed and Paul revolted, saying, "Ye observe days, and months, and times, and years. I am afraid of you, lest I have bestowed upon you labor in vain."

This antilegalist spirit has come down through the Christian ages in unbroken succession, warning against the detailed observances of the letter of old laws. The Church Universal owes a debt to its prophets who, in warning against lifeless formalism, have gone the limit of attempting total abolition of forms. The reform of formalism is a continual necessity.

Yet the inward experience must have some outward form of expression. Even the freest faiths, as we have seen, make a symbolism of their silences, a sacrament of guidance, and must necessarily set aside stated times for stated meetings. For them, as well as for the rest of Christendom, the Sundays of the year follow one another with mathematical reiteration. And they come at last to reclaim many of the forms they once discarded.

A clear understanding of the nature of symbolism would answer many of the objections advanced by Protestants against the acceptance of a better ordered calendar. For the calendar and all its component parts are symbols. To treat the symbol as though it were the reality is idolatry; to discard all symbolism because of former abuse is unrealism. "The form of religion," said Joseph Butler, "may indeed be where there is little of the thing itself, but the thing itself cannot be preserved amongst mankind without the form. Religion, through outward forms and ceremonies, mixes itself with business, civil forms, diversions, domestic entertainments, and every part of common life."

It may be that Phillips Brooks had some such meaning in mind in saying, "The Christian year preserves the personality of religion," for it would be as hard to think of Christianity without its body of practices as of a personality without its physical means of expression.

Pope Gregory the Great, writing to Augustine of England, stated the principle that has guided the Church through the ages on matters of form: "We do not honor good things because they are in certain places, but we honor places be-

cause of the things." The same might be said of special times
as well. Those who reject empty formalism have the prophets
and apostles on their side; but to reject the fact of time
and space is a denial of natural and social reality, and as
futile as it would be to discard preaching because man's
word is not God's Word.

Four Guiding Principles: Reiteration

Four guiding principles are seen in the development of
the Christian Year.

The principle of reiteration recognizes that religious
constancy comes through faithful repetition. "He prays
without ceasing," wrote Augustine of Hippo, "who prays
at fixed intervals." There is an element of self-delusion in
those who think they are more constant in their memorials
if they neglect the anniversaries. The criticism that celebrations confine the religious attitude to "one day only" is
not well founded. We are not less faithful to the continuing
sanctity of marriage, for instance, because we remember our
wedding anniversaries. The real deception is that, without
the special occasions, we forget while thinking we remember
"the year round." As proficiency in any skill calls for countless repetitions of performance, so the development of true
devotional attitudes is by a succession of observances brought
toward perfection. Augustine stated: "By festival solemnities
and set days we dedicate and sanctify to God the memory of
his benefits, lest unthankful forgetfulness should creep upon
us in course of time." And Hooker applied the same to
every phase of life: "Duties of all sorts must necessarily have
their several successions and seasons."

Appropriateness

The principle of appropriateness runs throughout the
Christian Year. The mystic William Law showed the value
of this principle as applied to the individual's prayer life,
regularly organized around the monastic offices and prefer-

ably observed in some habitual place. An accumulation of associations gathers about the particular prayer theme, regularly evoked on a particular time and in a particular place. And it follows that the opposite attitude becomes increasingly inappropriate, at least for the period of devotion. A "murder in a cathedral" seems more shocking than one in a tavern, since the former is dedicated in a special way to religion. As at the altar of private prayer or in the public holy place, a certain spiritual psychology of association is at work, so the stated observance of religion gathers to itself a special character.

Even in social life this principle is universally accepted, and not even the most spontaneous persons would expect to go ahead with the planned cocktail party on the eve of a loved one's funeral, but would decently recognize that "to every thing there is a season, and a time to every purpose under the heaven."

A fuller statement of this element of appropriateness which guides the practices of ceremonial religion, is in Ecclesiasticus (33:7-12):

> Why doth one day excel another, when as all the light of every day of the year is of the sun? By the knowledge of the Lord they were distinguished: and he altered seasons and feasts. Some of them hath he made high days, and hallowed them, and some of them hath he made ordinary days. And all men are from the ground, and Adam was created of earth. In much knowledge the Lord hath divided them, and made their ways diverse. Some of them hath he blessed and exalted, and some of them hath he sanctified, and set near himself.

Thus the divine act itself made for the difference of days and established the principle of appropriateness.

Separation

The principle of separation between sacred and profane has been followed through the whole development of the Christian Year. The sanctities of God are in the world but

76

not of it. They impinge upon the common life while not being absorbed by it. Both the separation and the impingement are necessary to redemption. Religion saves not by merely resembling the prevailing culture which is the objective of its redemptive concern but by being unlike that culture and, while remaining in it, standing above it as high inspiration and moral criticism. To point out the possibility of the corruption of this principle of separation is not to dispose of its necessity. Not forgetting the evil that issued from the medieval idea of holy orders as setting the clergy apart into a privileged class, we nonetheless still ordain clergy, recognizing their separation from the common life in their very dedication to its service. This separation is also recognized in the dedication of churches, the consecration of children, the baptism of adults, and the offering of some portion of worldly goods. It has deep ethical and social meanings as well as ceremonial significance. requiring of the faithful the full moral service which is the fruit of holiness.

Preparation

And religious preparation is a running theme throughout the Christian Year. Inherited from earliest times is this sense of the importance of the coming event, an importance requiring of the devotee a full and complete preparation of mind and spirit. Selden misses this point, seeing in the rhythm of the occasions the idea of withholding and giving, rather than that of preparation and performance. "What the Church debars us one day," he wrote, "she gives us leave to take out in another. First, we fast, and then we feast; first there is a Carnival, and then a Lent." The reason for this rhythm, however, is not simply to give relief after denial but rather to prepare for the coming event, as confession precedes communion. And so every memorial of Christian devotion is preceded by a period of fitting cultivation in which the mind and spirit are properly prepared for genuine participation. Advent is the spiritual preparation for Christmas as

Lent is for Easter, and even pre-Lent for Lent. And the principle of preparation is brought down into the worship of the week, whether in the Jewish service of separation, in the Catholic fast day, or in "The Cotter's Saturday Night" of Robert Burns.

Modern Protestants would do well not to despise these humble practices, and would find their worship immensely enhanced if preceded by proper devotions.

Much more time is given to preparation than to festivals in the Christian Year, as illustrated in the proportion between Advent and Christmastide. The whole year may be seen as continual preparation for the coming religious event, which frequently takes one high day following a long season of rigorous self-examination and mental conditioning.

Chapter V

CEREMONIAL ELABORATION

Fʀᴏᴍ this beginning the ceremonial Christian Year immediately began to grow toward its full elaboration, and by the latter part of the fourth century its entire framework had been established substantially as it remains to this day. We have suggested the probable order of appearance of the main events. The development was rapid, yet the separate observances have no official dates of beginning by which they may be plainly marked. They arrive in parallel or overlapping lines, the celebration usually beginning as a local custom, later taking on universal character, and finally, after considerable time, becoming official.

J. C. Shairp differentiates between the local and the catholic—or universal—occasions, the latter, "though not observed in all the churches, are yet memorials of the sacred facts by which Christians live." Their catholicity depends not on their universal keeping but on the nature of their teaching. Other days arise on special call in time of calamity or rejoicing or as memorials of exceptional events.

The probable order of main development was: Easter, Pentecost, Ascension Day, Epiphany, and Christmas.

Easter and Days Dependent

The clear fact is that Easter and days dependent upon it developed some time before Christmas and its associated days. Easter priority was natural in its being an adaptation of the ancient Passover, as yet a live tradition. This close association is seen in the name of the Christian high holiday Pascha, still used in the older churches. The word "Easter" is relatively late, being the Old English adaptation of *Eastre,* the name of the Teutonic goddess of spring and dawn. The Christian Paschal Feast was simply the elevation of the Lord's Day to an annual celebration, the "Sunday of Sundays." Again, the death and resurrection of Christ were of greater importance to the early Christians than his birth. The whole proclamation of the emerging Church revolves around the victory cry, "He who was crucified is risen!" It was natural that this primary witness of the Early Church should form its earliest festival. This priority of Easter in the thought of the Early Church is illustrated in the fact that three fourths of the entire Christian Year still turns around the Easter pole, from Septuagesima Sunday to the end of the Trinity season, while one fourth turns around Christmas.

This observation began very soon after the close of New Testament times. It is mentioned by Polycarp, a disciple of the Apostle John. The earliest of the Fathers refer to its celebration in Rome, although it falls on a variety of dates. The festival originally included observance of the Crucifixion as well as the Resurrection, and was the proper occasion for baptisms.

The English *Book of Common Prayer* gives the designation, "Easter Day on which the rest depend." As we shall later see, introduction of other days followed its lead, their places upon the calendar being related to Easter as the original events were related to the Resurrection.

Staley sums up the meaning of this high day:

The halo surrounding the weekly memorial of the Lord spread itself out in the greater glory of the annual remembrance of Him at the Easter festival. Easter was to the Sundays of the year as a star differing from all other stars in glory. Thus the weekly commemoration of Jesus found its development in the yearly observance of Easter; whilst from the observation of Easter and the association therewith, other commemorations followed.

This first of the high festivals of Christianity is still the principal celebration of the Christian Year in all branches

of the Universal Church. While there remain, in the Southern states, a few scattered fellowships holding doggedly to the dissenting tradition of "No Easter," observance of the day is all but unanimous throughout Christendom; and it is also a gala folk day in the cultural life of nearly every nation. The Catholic missal recalls that St. Leo referred to Easter as "the feast of feasts," saying that Christmas was a preparation for this central "Sunday of Sundays."

In all churches Easter is a proper time for the Holy Communion, although where this is observed on Maundy Thursday it is usually not repeated in the nonliturgical churches on Easter Day. A wider Protestant usage is the reception of confirmants and other candidates for membership. Traditionally baptisms were held on this feast and on Pentecost.

The early Christians adopted existing folk spring festival customs into the celebration of the day. These took their origin in the natural life of primitive peoples in response to the seasonal rhythm of life. Christianity thus extends to the spiritual power, a natural aspect of life, and converts the rhythmic recurrence of spring, with its flow of new life, into the immortality of those who, believing in Him, "shall never die."

Wilson called Easter "the summit of the Christian Year."

81

Pentecost

The chief day dependent upon Easter is the Christian Pentecost, fifty days after Easter, as the Jewish institution was fifty after the Passover. This celebration originated almost at the same time as the Easter custom.

※ Its rise follows the same logic as that of the Feast of Easter in that it also comes from an antecedent Jewish tradition which is adapted to the uses of Christians. It, too, fell on a Sunday when the Holy Spirit came upon the multitude, and heaven, speaking with tongues of fire, proclaimed the Church of Christ. This traditional origin as related in the book of Acts developed into a stated celebration with the entrance of the Christian mind into missionary consciousness. It is popularly called the "Birthday of the Church," although the Church existed prior to Pentecost, its true beginnings being found in the congregation of Israel.

※ The English designation "Whitsunday" for this celebration means simply "white Sunday," from the baptismal robes of the candidates (the altar color for the day being red). It was erroneously believed in earlier times that this name came from "wit" and was supposed to connote the Spirit's gift of wit, or wisdom, to the Church.

The red of Pentecost, the color of blood and fire, is the sign of the Church and its martyrs. It is on the heroic note that the great celebration of the day begins, with the Introit:

"The Spirit of the Lord hath filled the whole earth." The birthday of the Church is observed with exultation, the unity of the Church is sought in prayer, the triumph of the Church is proclaimed, and all the holy offices are appropriate on this day. Communicants may be received; the communion celebrated, baptisms administered, and ordinations conferred.

Pentecost has always been an outstanding celebration of the Church militant. The attributes of God as energizer, conveyor of power, and vigorous worker are stressed, together with the comfort of the Spirit. "The formal launching of the Church upon its world-wide mission" is accomplished by the marching hymns of Christianity and with stirring symbolism. The "rushing of a mighty wind" is represented by trumpets and the "tongues like as of fire" by torches, or sometimes by rose leaves sprinkled upon the congregation, in the liturgical churches. Its strategic position in the Church Year is illustrated by the fact that the older churches count the following Sundays as Sundays "after Pentecost," whereas the younger churches (Lutheran and Anglican) measure "after Trinity."

The Greek influence on the Jews is reflected in the name "Pentecost," coming from the Greek word meaning "fifty." As the Jewish Pentecost was fifty days after the Passover, the Christian Pentecost remains fifty days after Easter, the first forty days being those spent by Christ between the Resurrection and the Ascension and the remaining ten the time the apostles waited for the coming of the Spirit.

Franz Werfel, in *Embezzled Heaven,* gives the spirit of this important day and its season:

Whitsuntide was perhaps the most joyful of all the feasts of exultation, for it proclaimed the universal language of the fiery tongues, the descent of the Holy Ghost upon earth, and was not linked, like Christmas and Easter, with the journey of mankind from birth, along the path of suffering, to death. Like the sun, the Church was entering the season of its greatest triumph, for on this day, when spring, the begetter, was pressing on towards summer, which brought forth the fruits, the *spiritus sanctus* assumed royal dominion over the universe.[1]

The Protestant denominations and the Federal Council are strongly reviving the full use of this day, with appropri-

[1] New York: The Viking Press, 1940. Used by permission.

ate services and aids to private meditation, the predominant theme being that of the unity of the Church.

Ascension Day

As Pentecost marks the biblical fifty days from the Resurrection to the visitation of the Spirit, so Holy Thursday, or

Ascension Day, recognizes the biblical forty days between Easter and the Ascent. Augustine records its general establishment by the fourth century. Also, in Sylvia's *Pilgrimage* is a description of the solemn procession which on that day went up the Mount of Olives, where Constantine's mother, the Empress Helena, had built a church.

"The last in sequence of our Lord's commemorations," this day recalls the marvelous scene as recorded in the book of Acts: "As they were looking, he was taken up; and a cloud received him out of their sight." It is one of the neglected days of Christian observance in that it falls on a weekday. Yet it deals with one of the most significant aspects of Christian teaching, its cosmic meaning. The Risen Christ is bound no longer by earth ties. He takes his eternal place at the right hand of the Father in heaven; his everlasting manhood and saviourhood are celebrated in the day commemorating this miraculous ascent. As Judge of the quick and the dead, King of all kings and Lord of all lords, he is honored and obeyed; and petitions are addressed to him who, as Great High Priest and Intercessor, possesses all power in heaven and on earth.

Since the celebration falls upon a weekday, its spirit is

continued the following Sunday, called Ascension Sunday, or Expectation Sunday, when the Holy Communion is especially appropriate, with its emphasis upon the divine presence and upon the commemorative. Our own ascension is also implied in the prayers, "that we may also in heart and mind thither ascend, and with him continually dwell."

Frank E. Wilson characterized the day: "So does the Christian year reach a magnificent crescendo. . . . The Ascension season is the link between Christ's earthly ministry and the Church (his ongoing ministry)."

In Catholicism this day ranks in importance with the feasts of Easter and Pentecost. During the service the paschal candle, which has burned the forty days since Easter, is extinguished.

The Epiphany

The Epiphany began in the Eastern Church, probably among the Jewish Christians, and originally commemorated the baptism of our Lord. It was referred to by Ephraem the Syrian, A.D. 373, as the Feast of the Baptism of Christ. It was later associated with the Nativity, with special reference to the visitation of the Magi, and is still called "Old Christ-

mas." In the West the day retains the significance of the manifestation of the universal Christ to the wise men of the East, who have come to symbolize the whole world; and the day marks the beginning of the missionary season of the Church.

The meaning of the word "Epiphany" is "manifestation"; and in the Eastern Church "Theophany," or "God's manifestation," is its interchangeable term. Besides the Baptism and the visit of the wise men, the miracle of the marriage supper at Cana is also an early theme of the day, although the Western Church from the fifth century specialized on the Magi. Augustine left six Epiphany sermons, all stressing the visit of the Magi, as did also St. Leo's eight sermons— for example, in *"Solemnitati Epiphaniae"*: "The day on which Christ, the Saviour of the world, first appeared to the Gentiles, is to be reverenced by us, dearly beloved, with sacred honor; and we ought to feel this day in our hearts those joys which were in the hearts of the three Magi, when being urged onward by the sign and leading of a new star."

According to an old English custom, the sovereign offered gold, frankincense, and myrrh at the altar.

Efforts have been made by many astronomers to account for the Epiphany star. Johannes Kepler four centuries ago discovered a certain conjunction of planets which occurs every eight hundred years, and calculated one such at the time of the Saviour's birth. Egyptian records later discovered are said to have corroborated this evidence, yet the matter is still one of conjecture.

The Magi were a priestly class in Persia who dealt in astronomy and in the mysteries of occultism. They were the scientists of their day, the sort who began calendars. Legends concerning the biblical wise men are many and varied. The names Caspar, Melchior, and Balthazzar are purely traditional, yet the "remains" of these men are to be viewed in the cathedral of Cologne. The only gospel reference is in the short sentence, "There came wise men from the east."

But these mythological characters have become a symbol for the knowledge and wealth of the whole world, which now comes under the province of the incarnate Son of God. The shepherds, too, are part of the manifestation of the Word to the lowly.

A doctrinal consideration entered into the change of the birth celebration from January 6 to December 25. The "adoptionist heresy" held that Christ's divinity came from the baptism, while the main line of Christian teaching held that he was divine from the birth. And so it was that the separation of the birth from the baptism, to save the former from eclipse by the latter, became one of the motives for change. In the present Church Year, as observed by Western Christianity, Epiphany is retained as the day of the Magi and given the popular designation "Twelfth Day."

Christmas

The celebration of Christmas as the birthday of our Lord is also one of the captures of the pagan institutions by Christians. Besides having the doctrinal motive as related above, it was evidently introduced with the conscious purpose of crowding out the corrupt celebrations of the winter solstice and Mithraic festivals to the sun, with the supplanting of the physical sun by Christ, the Light of the World. The winter solstice was erroneously calculated at December 25 in the Julian calendar. The birthdays of at least five ancient gods are placed on this date.

Because of the importance of the event marked by Christmas, the day became the second great peak of the Christian Year.

While we do not know the exact origin of this observance, the writings of the Fathers are full of references to it, and even at early dates they point to its having been for some time in existence. It is likely it began as a local custom somewhere in Egypt, and later spread over the whole Church. Chrysostom in A.D. 388, at Antioch, referred to the Feast of the Nativity as having been celebrated in the East ten years previously. It was, no doubt, in that year that he introduced it at Rome. But we have read of its having been in Egypt in the second century, although Hastings does not find it in Alexandria until between A.D. 400 and 432. Its course, coming as a local custom from somewhere in Egypt, seems to have led to Antioch, Rome, Constantinople, Alexandria, and finally Jerusalem.

Originally the celebration was called "Christ's Mass"; the term "Christmas" did not come into use until the twelfth century.

It is unnecessary here to expand upon the significance of the day, so familiar to all Christians as one of the two outstanding events in their religious calendar. Even more than Easter, it has taken on a general cultural character as well as a religious; and customs from all lands have been added to its enrichment as a folk festival. The Romans gave presents at the winter celebrations, and the Christians continued the custom in recognition of God's gift of his Son. Germany contributed the evergreen tree as a symbol of everlasting life. The Druids gave their sacred mistletoe, with healing powers, appropriate emblem of him who was "the healing of the nations." The holly, representing the crown of thorns with drops of blood, came from Merry England. The yule log, receiving into its bright flames the hatreds and distrusts of the past year, came from Scandinavia. Firecrackers at Christmas are a custom of some parts of our South, as well as of China. Bells, lights, and other usual symbols occur everywhere. An old legend says that a candle in the window will light the way of the Christ Child home. Holland is remembered in the children's St. Nicholas, whose name became "Santa Claus." Although his original day, December 6, remains in the Catholic saints' list, it was changed to December 25 by English custom. The day also gives a theme to music, from the gentle carols to the great cantatas and oratorios of the masters, and to religious art.

The two conspicuous events, Christmas and Easter, form the poles, or focuses, of the whole Ecclesiastical Year, one marking the birth, the other the resurrection of our Lord, one celebrating the winter, the other the spring—the preparation for and the fulfillment of redemption.

The Determination of Times

Several considerations were in the minds of the Church Fathers in making the decisions as to the proper times of celebrations, their relationship to each other, and the distances between them. Historic accuracy is the least among these considerations, there being as yet no historic apparatus in the modern sense.

The New Testament source was important in giving the proper day of the week and the association with Jewish ceremonials, although little help is given from this source on accurate datings. Thus, though the New Testament fixes Easter on a Sunday and associates it with the Passover, it was well into the fourth century before the date was finally determined; and the echoes of the controversy around it continued for several more centuries. We shall see the story of that controversy in a special place.

Doctrinal considerations entered in—as, for instance, in the case of the separation of Christmas from Epiphany, which separation was in part the answer of the Western Church to the "adoptionist heresy."

Competition with other religious cultures affected the decisions, notably in the case of Christmas as a Christian check on the pagan Mithraic festivals and of the Feast of Circumcision as an answer to the Roman New Year orgies. A measure of competition with Judaism is shown in the Easter controversy.

The universality and unity of the Church was a strong motive in getting a final settlement of dates which would be acceptable throughout Christendom. Direct appeal to this motive is heard through all the discussions and councils. Time and again the argument calls for unity of acceptance, though that unity be had at the expense of historic accuracy. Christopher Clavius remarked that the Church "cares more for peace and uniformity than she does for equinox and new moon."

A "plan of the ages," widely accepted in the third century, had an influence, particularly on the determination of the Christmas date. This was the belief that the Creation took place on the spring equinox, and that the "new Creation" fell on the winter solstice. This was one of the arguments by which the Nativity was fixed on December 25, and later the Annunciation on March 25.

Natural intervals between events were also considered—as, for instance, the nine months between the conception and birth of our Lord. And there were also customary intervals, notably the time before the circumcision, coming on the octave of the birth, according to Jewish custom—at which time the child's name was conferred—and the period before the purification, the Jewish antecedent to the "churching of women," which came within forty days after the birth. There were also traditional or historical intervals, such as that between Easter and Ascension Day. Thus the establishment of one controlling date automatically set others in relation to itself.

Symbolic significance was also considered—as, for instance, in the forty days of Lent being representative of the forty days' fast in the wilderness, or the forty hours in the tomb.

Only last in importance came the question of historical accuracy, later arguments along this line usually being brought in to reinforce a position already taken. The Easter controversy produced reams of writing seeking to "prove" the exact date of the original Easter; but these were advanced by persons who obviously had other motives first—for instance, the unity of the Church or an anti-Jewish bias.

These considerations were important in the minds of the early Fathers as they were giving uniqueness to their new-found faith.

The Principle of Preparation and the Joining of Seasons

Need for preparation for every religious event was second nature to the Christians, having been inherited along with the Jewish traditions. The Jews observed a day of preparation before every holy day, and a special preparatory service on Friday preceded each Sabbath worship. Every coming religious event had its proper means of making ready. We are not surprised, therefore, to find that the great seasons of preparation appeared in the Christian calendar shortly after the appearance of the main ceremonials. Easter almost from the first was a season rather than a single day, originally including the memorial of the death as well as the celebration of the resurrection, in a forty-hour observance in token of the time Jesus spent in the tomb. A little later the Easter motif ruled from Palm Sunday to Pentecost. Holy Week is referred to in the Apostolic Constitutions in the third century. The pre-Easter season was later extended to thirty days, and finally, by the Nicene Council, to the full forty days. Athanasius on a trip to Europe found not only Lent but also Holy Week in full devotional use, and upon his return to Egypt he urged a stricter fast upon his people "lest they become a laughingstock." Pope Gregory I established Ash

Wednesday in the sixth century as the beginning day of preparation.

From Ash Wednesday to Easter Eve is the **Quadragesi**-ma season, or English *Lent* (from the Anglo-Saxon *lencthen*,

meaning "spring"), as observed today as the preparation of the faithful for the proper celebration of Easter. The forty days are symbolic of the time spent by Moses on Mount Sinai, the forty years' wanderings in the wilderness, the forty days' temptation of our Lord, or his forty hours in the tomb. Since Sunday is always a feast day, only weekdays are counted. The designation "Sundays *in* Lent" indicates that the Sundays are not properly part of the Lenten fast.

The disciplinary use of the period is urged by Gregory the Great:

From this day [Ash Wednesday] unto the joys of the Paschal solemnity there are six weeks coming . . . that we, who through the past year have lived too much for ourselves, should mortify ourselves to our Creator in the tenth of the year through abstinence. Whence, most dear brethren, as ye are bid by the law to offer the tenths of your substance, so contend to offer to him also the tenth of your days.

Holy Week, immediately preceding Easter, was from the first observed as an intensive commemoration of the sufferings of our Lord. "It is," wrote Staley, "a mirror reflecting in orderly sequence and detail the Passion of our Saviour."

There has been some confusion in the use of the term "Passion" in connection with this week. Passiontide is the full two weeks' period from Passion Sunday to Easter Eve, and Passion Week is the week preceding Holy Week. The week beginning with Palm Sunday is Holy Week—or, in the Greek Church, Great Week. Each day of this week is especially designated to the use suggested by the events recorded in Scripture. Through the week, the final intensive preparation of penitence is accomplished in anticipation of Easter Day.

Next, a period of preparation for the preparation was added in the *pre-Lenten Sundays,* Septuagesima, Sexagesima, and Quinquagesima, the words standing roughly for seventy, sixty, and fifty days before Easter, respectively, or, more accurately, for the Sundays in the respective decades of days. This short season was added late, probably to complete the joining of seasons by covering the break between Epiphany season and Lent. In current Protestant use this brief season is sometimes omitted, its Sundays being added to the Epiphany season.

For the liturgical churches, "the pre-Lenten Sundays impress upon the Christian the necessity of stiffening spiritual determination in anticipation of the self-imposed restrictions which must be faced in the Lenten season," says Frank E. Wilson.

Easter is considered the first Sunday of *Eastertide,* or the Paschal Time, which extends through the forty days to Ascension Day.

Pentecost also grew early from a day to a season, although in this case the thought was not preparation but the continuing march of the Church, militant and triumphant. Whitsuntide, or the season of Pentecost proper, has had various definitions of limits, but in present Catholic use it extends the Pentecost theme through the entire second half of the Church Year. Until Advent, Sundays are designated "Sundays after Pentecost." There may be as many as twenty-eight and as

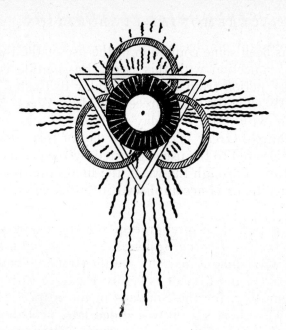

few as twenty-three Sundays after Pentecost, depending upon the date of Easter. Whitsuntide proper extends only from the Day of Pentecost to the end of the week.

Trinity Sunday was first observed by Thomas à Becket, and its use spread from Canterbury. The designation "Sundays after Trinity" was thus English in origin, and the day itself was not regularized for the whole Catholic Church until A.D. 1334, when Pope John XXII ordered the feast for the entire Church on the Sunday following Pentecost, the reason for the position on the calendar being that the doctrine was originally given following the Pentecost experience.

This difference in the counting of the Sundays of the second half year is the most conspicuous disparity between the Catholic Church and the Anglican and Lutheran. While it seems unlikely that it represents a deliberate breach within the ecumenical Church, it does show an important lack of agreement, similar to the earlier usages concerning Easter. The Catholic emphasis for the second half, thus, falls on the Church, which received its world-wide charter at Pentecost.

The Protestant emphasis is upon God, as conveyed in the classic formula of the Holy Trinity.

Advent, recognizing the same principle of preparation, appears late. We have already referred to Sylvia's *Pilgrimage* as one of the early sources. Sylvia, in A.D. 380, made a trip from Spain to Rome and Palestine, on her return writing this interesting account of the celebrations she had witnessed. She makes no reference to Advent, although the time of her trip included the winter season. The period is found in Gaul and Spain by the fifth century, and it seems to have begun locally as congregations felt the need for Christmas preparation. The variety of customs thus arising was later harmonized into the present scheme. The beginning of Advent is generally described as "the Sunday nearest St. Andrew's Day," which falls on November 30; its close is on Christmas Eve.

This is the New Year season of the Church Year, "the vestibule to the temple of His presence." As "winter Lent," it offers the faithful an opportunity for preparation for the coming birth of Christ. Its themes are: the coming of Christ as a babe; his second advent, when he shall reign over the whole earth; and his *continual* coming into the hearts that "prepare him room." All the rituals emphasize the doctrine of the Incarnation, and each Sunday has its separate emphasis. The coming of the Christ is proclaimed in the Creation, in the Bible, in the Prophets, and by John the Baptist.

This season looks backward and forward, back to the Creation, and forward to the New Creation. "Jesus Christ and the apostles," said Pascal, "taught us that there would be two advents, one in lowliness to humble the proud, the other in glory to exalt the humble."

The earlier variety of uses of this season is still reflected in the manner of observance at the Church of Milan, where Advent is observed from Martinmas, November 11.

The Catholic designation is "Sundays of Advent"; the Lutheran-Anglican is "Sundays *in* Advent."

The spirit of the season is summed up by Dom Cabrol:

> It is the near approach of the Son of God in the flesh for which one must prepare oneself with greater watchfulness, and by the practice of works of charity; it is the voice of the prophets announcing the Messiah who comes; it is the world awaiting its Redeemer, sighing as the parched ground for the dew of heaven; it is St. Paul exhorting the faithful, awakening them from their sleep upon the vigil of the Coming of Christ; it is John the Baptist, the last of the long line of prophets, who cries in the wilderness, "Prepare ye the way of the Lord!"

In the other direction, the *Epiphany* grew to a season, the Sundays after Epiphany being from one to six, depending on the date of Easter. This is the season of missionary emphasis, in keeping with the manifestation to the Gentiles.

The three traditional "manifestations" are: (1) to the wise men of the East, (2) in the Baptism, and (3) at the marriage supper of Cana in Galilee. To these are added the themes that complete the season.

Thus, by introduction of periods of preparation and by extension of celebrations, the Christian Year joined its seasons around the calendar. The completed scheme offers an unbroken drama of the chief events of the life of our Lord and of the religion he founded. It moves with logic through the rhythms of the natural year; and the individual Christian, by participation, becomes an actor in the pageant of God.

In the first half of the year God reveals himself to man; in the second half, man responds to the revelation of God. The first half contains the major *events* of Christ's life, as disclosures of the nature of God; the second half contains the major *teachings* of the Christian life, to enable man to conform to the divine will.

The Christian Year begins the first Sunday in Advent, the Sunday nearest St. Andrew's Day, November 30. On this "Christian New Year" the works of creation are sung, and the season of preparation for the coming of our Lord is ushered in with solemn joy. Then comes the great celebration of the Nativity and the Incarnation, with Christmastide usually occupying two Sundays. Epiphany and its Sundays proclaim the manifestation of the universal Christ to all the nations, to all conditions of men and all provinces of life. The pre-Lenten Sundays concentrate on the Christian virtues faith, hope, and love, as fitting preparation for Lent. Lent, the following forty days, is the Church's profoundest period for personal examination and repentance, reaching the very depth of contrition in Holy Week. Each day of that great week has a special significance assigned in the gospel accounts, as Christ moves with the dignity of divinity from the triumph of Palm Sunday to the humiliation of Good Friday. Lent closes Saturday noon.

Then—

> Easter Day breaks!
> Christ rises! Mercy every way
> Is Infinite—and who can say?

Easter is not the close of Lent, but the beginning of Eastertide; and the triumphant joy of the season continues to Ascension Day, forty days later. Ascensiontide we have seen as the celebration of Christ's cosmic significance as he now "sits at the right hand of God the Father" and as a period of preparation for the coming Pentecost. The close of Ascensiontide ends the first half of the Christian Year.

The second half of the year continues to its close on the Sunday next before Advent. This long period of the march of the Church Triumphant emphasizes the human response to the divine commands.

Fasting and Feasting

The rhythm between preparation and celebration is marked by the alternate fasting and feasting that runs through the whole year. The origin of these customs as expressions of religious feeling goes back to primitive times.

Fasting is assumed to have begun in the natural physical repugnance to food under emotional stress or excitement. At first involuntary, it later takes on the character of conscious abstention in time of mourning or under impending threat. It is later associated with the dualistic view which regards the body as evil and sees in its deprivation a means of purifying the soul. This idea carried over into the Christian view for many centuries, and is prominent in some forms of asceticism. Jesus himself fasted, but his fasts were the natural accompaniment of periods of absorbed preoccupation. That he held the stated observances lightly is evidenced by the accusation that "thy disciples fast not."

The earliest Christian stated days for fasting were established by Montanus in the middle of the second century. At first Wednesdays and Fridays were set apart as "stations," the name being borrowed from the language of soldiery; these were the days preparatory to the Sunday worship, when the Christian stood sentinel. Wednesday was later dropped and Friday has been continued as the classic Christian fast day. The usage does not require complete abstention from food, but merely a limited diet with meat forbidden.

Through the Church Year there are also fasting seasons. These are the times of general penitence or of preparation for a coming festival. These seasons are called *tempora claustra*—"closed times"—during which certain practices are inappropriate or forbidden. For instance, marriages were forbidden from Christmas to Epiphany and from Ash Wednesday to Easter.

Feasting is a very ancient means of communal celebration. The meal has always been a common bond for the family or tribe. The feast of the first fruits is practically universal as a means of rejoicing, or appeasing the spirits and guaranteeing crops.

In all societies feasting is associated with such major events as birth, induction into society, marriage, victory in war, change of rulers, the advent of the seasons, and commemorations. We have seen that the Christian Year began with the breaking of bread around a common table. That Jesus heartily approved the fellowship aspect of life is shown again in the fact that he was accused of being "gluttonous, and a winebibber."

The early Christian meal set the precedent for the more elaborate annual festivals later to come. All the high holidays of the year are feasts, and their seasons continue the festival spirit. Sometimes the real character of a celebration was a matter of debate, as in the case of the Feast of Circumcision, there having been a controversy of wide extent over whether the day should be a fast or a feast. It was not settled as a feast until the sixth century.

The elements of festival days, according to Christian teaching, are praise, bounty, and rest; and Gloria in Excelsis is the theme of all. As fasting may be turned to abuse, so may the practice of feasting; hence Hooker issued a warning: "But, when converted to worship of false gods, songs of praise were idolatry, bounty excess, and their rest wantonness."

Symbolic significance is added to these changing seasons in the posture of prayer, standing being the mode at feasts, while kneeling is proper for fasts. The ecclesiastical colors also mark the changes of season and of mood. White, the color of the Godhead, represents the purity, joy, and victory of the high days and seasons, running through Christmastide, Eastertide, Ascensiontide, and Corpus Christi Day. Green stands for life and growth, and is used through the Epiphany and Trinity seasons (except for the white of Corpus Christi Day and near Sundays, and the fifteenth Sunday after Pentecost in Catholic usage). Purple, or violet, is the color of penitence, used in Advent and Lent. (The pre-Lenten season may use either green or purple.) Red, the color of blood and fire, is the sign of the Church and its martyrs. It is used in Whitsuntide and on all the saints' days. On Good Friday the altar is draped in black; on other occasions no color at all is used, the altar being bare.

The Principle of Separation and the Conflict of Cultures

We have noted the principle of "separation" involved in all cultural and religious calendars. Cultural and even political conflicts are given the value of absoluteness and become struggles between the holy and the profane. In this early period Christianity shows in its developing calendar the reactions against both Rome and the Jews. The early hope of Jewish acceptance of the Messiah by conversion en masse waned, and was finally despaired of. The natural response was one of opposition. The destruction of the Temple by Titus in the Jewish war of A.D. 70 offered additional opportunity for the Christian mission to the Jews, and this mission was meeting with success. At the same time Paul was apostle to the Gentiles. The conflict between Jews and Christians entered into the Christian community itself, reaching the proportions of the Pauline controversy with the Judaizing Christians. The issue focused on the ceremonial formality of circumcision. Paul's point of view prevailed, and the principle of Christian universalism was established along with freedom from the old law. Stalker gave important place to this universalism as perhaps the chief cause of the breach between the early Christians and the provincial Jews. The issue was not finally laid with Paul's victory over Peter, but reappeared in violent form with the Ebionites and Nazarenes around A.D. 200, the former being the Judaizers of the rigid and aloof variety—the Pharisaical Christians of marked hostility to the Gentile converts—while the latter, though milder in their attitude, continued the Jewish practices for themselves. In this contest the prevailing side was that of the separation of the new Christian culture from its Jewish origins and associations. Something distinctly new was to come forth, and the story of this struggle and its outcome is recorded in ceremonial observances.

We have already seen that the contest between Christianity and the pagan culture of Rome revolved largely around the public observances. Let it be remembered that Rome's religious policy was one of tolerance. All religions were welcome additions to the eclectic religion of Rome. Far from forcing their varied peoples to accept a common state faith, Rome on the other hand required them to be faithful to their mother faith. She then sought to incorporate the mother faith into the service of the state. Christianity might have lived peaceably in the Roman Empire had it remained a sect of Jews. But its separation from Judaism, plus its zeal to convert the pagans, provoked the opposition of Rome.

Opposition was drawn by A.D. 64, under Nero, whose persecutions are reflected in the late New Testament portions. At this time the charge lodged against Christians was "arson." By A.D. 90 the name itself had become criminal, although there was no general persecution until about the middle of the third century. By then the charges included atheism, anarchism, and even cannibalism and incest. The origin of these attacks seems to have been with the people rather than with the government, the emperors acting officially only after being spurred on by mob violence. The Christians, meeting this opposition, struggled back with the weapons at their disposal, using against the enemy not only the "sword of truth and the breastplate of righteousness" but also the instrumentality of religious celebrations—for example, the placing of Christmas and the Feast of the Circumcision so as to offer maximum competition with the pagan rites. Ambrose expressed this motive: "We fast on this day [Circumcision] that the heathen may know we condemn their pleasures." And Augustine spoke in the same strain.

For all this opposition, Christianity was definitely influenced by pagan customs, incorporating some of them, such as the giving of gifts at Christmas time, into their own practices. And thoughout the history of the Christian Year is observed a tendency toward corruption and reversion to the pagan folkways. One illustration of this tendency is in the Feast of Fools, which came into popularity from the eleventh to the fifteenth centuries as a parody on the Mass, in the spirit of the Saturnalia, conducted by the subdeacons.

Rome was an all-inclusive organism which sought to absorb and adapt to its own use every foreign practice, rejecting with ruthlessness the practices she could not so utilize. The story of the "ten persecutions" belongs to the account of Christianity's gradual and painful separation from pagan culture. Despite these persecutions—perhaps because of them—the Christians became more and more a distinct and peculiar people, rejecting conformity at pain of death and effecting their own mode of life as seen concretely and dramatically in the Christian Year. The decline of the first faith was revived in the contest between spirit and flesh. The catacombs not only gave new insights, deeper courage, and radiant victory but also stimulated the development of symbolism as a sort of secret code between comrades of persecution. Justin, one of the first martyrs, wrote a good account of the early worship that was giving distinctiveness to the new faith against the totalitarian effort at absorption or extinction.

The Easter Controversy and the Council of Nicaea

The Nicene Council, called by Constantine in A.D. 325 to settle the Arian-Athanasian controversy, is a milestone in the development of the Christian calendar. It is not within our present purpose to discuss this controversy except in its bearing upon the calendar development. Arius and his followers held to the Unitarian idea of God and the human

idea of Jesus, while Athanasius and his company contended for the Trinitarian doctrine of God and the dual nature of Christ, human and divine. The debate threatened the unity of the Church and Empire as each side, in turn gaining ascendency, persecuted the opposition with exile and death. The emperor had no personal preference in the debate, but required the theologians to sit in council until a formula could be arrived at. In the stormy sessions Athanasius was victorious, and his victory gave the Church its trunk line of orthodoxy which was to continue through the Catholic tradition until now. The Nicene and Athanasian creeds were the later formal expression of this victory, taking their places, along with the Apostles' Creed, as the unifying symbols of Christianity. Every clause of these great statements may be related to some special day upon the Christian calendar. The doctrines advanced thus became concretely dramatized in the public celebrations.

With the settlement of this doctrinal dispute the Nicene Council also resolved another quarrel of long standing. This was the Easter controversy. The pagans had ridiculed the Christians for not being able to agree on the proper date of their chief festival. As early as the middle of the second century the churches of Asia and Rome had different practices in this regard, and Polycarp and Anicetus engaged in a historic conversation on the merits of their respective customs. Again, about A.D. 170 to 177 the Laodicean controversy dealt in an inconsequential way with the same question. In

A.D. 190 Bishop Victor of Rome and Polycrates were the principals in the argument, which had now reached serious proportions, with Victor excommunicating all the Asian churches and inviting a bitter reaction. Bishop Irenaeus of Lyons interceded for the Asians. This quarrel continued into the fourth century.

It would not be interesting to follow the many pages of reasoning and debate at Nicaea, and to do so would perhaps convince us that the Fathers spent a vast deal of time and lengthy locution upon a trivial matter. Suffice it to say that the issue was settled by action of an authoritative Church Council; and the Quartodecimans, or the Christians who had been celebrating Easter on the fourteenth day of Nissan, were ordered to accept the definition of the date which still holds: *"on the first Sunday after the full moon on or after the first day of spring, March 21, or, if the full moon is on Sunday, the next Sunday after."* This may be anywhere within a spread of thirty-five days, from March 22 to April 25, but with the extremes being reached very infrequently.

It is an intricate matter—hopeless if each Christian were to calculate his own Easter. Many writers have explained this dating in detail, but the Prayer Book tables are no easier than logarithms to handle. The simple advice of one writer is the best available on the question of the proper determination of Easter: "Buy a penny almanac."

The importance of this settlement will be seen as the story of the Christian Year develops. The Greek calendar prompted another controversy within Rome, which was settled A.D. 525. The Gallic Christians had another system which held from A.D. 457 to 800. And the matter was finally settled for England in A.D. 664.

Saints' Days

Informal celebrations of saints' days began probably with Montanus about A.D. 150. This was a practice later to be adopted officially and to become an integral part of the ceremonial year. Although many centuries were to pass before the heroes of the Church were canonized, there was shown respect from the beginning. Polycarp's martyrdom, February 23, A.D. 155, probably began the custom of observing the memory of the saints on their deathdays rather than on their birthdays. This was part and parcel of the era of persecution, with its glorification of suffering; and the deathdays were regarded as the time of birth into the Kingdom of Heaven. By the Diocletian persecutions a distinct martyrology was in vogue. The calendars of the third century give the deathdays of the apostles and the Christmas martyrs Stephen, John, and the "holy innocents"; the birthday of John the Baptist; and the conversion day of Paul. Prayers for the dead were customary by this time.

In A.D. 527 Dionysius Exiguus the Little, a monk at Rome, first marked off time by the birth of Christ, using the designations "A.C." and "A.D."—a sign of the important position Christianity had attained from its humble beginnings when the infant Lord was laid in the manger at Bethlehem. Though this designation was not used officially until the time of Charlemagne, the Church by now had the full equipment of a ceremonial year and was well on its advance toward a world-wide destiny. Each subsequent year of the coming centuries would be known as *anno Domini,* the "year of our Lord."

Chapter VI

CONQUEST AND CONVERSION

THE Christian Year by now has grown from New Testament beginnings to full elaboration, wresting its independence from the mother faith, securing its existence against the pagan superstitions, and finally, with the conversion of Constantine, winning official recognition of Rome. Its next historic tasks will be to make Rome the center of Christian culture and to convert the barbarians of the North.

Christian Universalism

The idea of universalism, apparent in Christianity from the first, grew to become the *catholic idea*. The word had been used from the middle of the second century, but with no more exact meaning than the word "universal." The universalism inherent in the teachings of Christ became articulate in ecclesiastical theory as the Christian community was forming into an organic whole. The movement was toward a common authority and discipline. Perhaps the earliest formulation of the catholic idea was in the middle of the third century when

Cyprian advanced the doctrine and established the prestige of the Roman Church as the seat of Christian authority. The great Augustine of Hippo died in A.D. 430, leaving such a weighty contribution to the theological structure of the rising Christianity as would assure its carrying to the Roman intellectuals and barbarian tribes a sound content of teaching, centering on the catholic conception of the Church.

Along with this, liturgical development had gone far toward universal imposition of ceremonies. The authority of the apostles was recognized, and many of the services were given their names. Through the Church four main liturgies had been adopted and regularized over the respective areas: the Oriental, the Alexandrian, the Gallican, and the Roman. An impressive beginning had been made on great choral and congregational music. The young Church was consolidating its position and acquiring such an equipment of symbol and ceremony as would make its approach to the unconverted attractive and intelligible.

Barbarians

The inroads of the barbarian tribes into the boundaries of the Empire foretold the final destruction of paganism and of the Empire itself. This outer force, aided by the inner decay of Roman culture, meant first the downfall of the pagan religion and afterward the decline and fall of the greatest political entity of the ancient world. After a series of maraudings by the Germanic tribes over a period of two centuries, "Alaric the Hun" administered the deathblow to paganism in A.D. 410; and the sack of the city followed in A.D. 469, with the barbarian Odoacer becoming king of Rome and the Christian Pope Gelasius his subject.

Even before the barbarian attacks, the Roman religion was in a period of progressive decay, and was retained by intellectuals and the rulers mainly as a means for keeping the masses in order. No man of standing would profess to believe in the gods. Religious discussions among the cultured never turned upon the question of truth, but only upon considerations of utility. Generally it was assumed that the gods were not real; the only remaining question was whether they were useful in conditioning the masses to purposes of state. Such gods could not long survive. Unbelief could not be held as a private possession of the elite; the masses, too, would question; and upon the rise of general skepticism the gods would lose the power which all along had depended upon the public superstition.

Whatever may be thought of the genuineness of Constantine's "conversion," his political prudence may not be doubted. The first of the emperors clearly to see that a nation's power, indeed its very existence, depends in the last analysis upon the vitality and validity of its religion, he officially adopted Christianity in an effort to meet the situation brought on by the decline of pagan faith, and thus set the Empire itself against its own pagan religion. This complete reversal of the Roman policy of tolerance added a strong factor to the decline of the old superstitions. Paganism would continue for a century, but its doom was sure. Not only did Constantine accept Christianity as it was, he also vigorously used the power of his office in furthering its universal claims and in

shaping its unity, as we saw in the account of the Nicene Council.

As the barbarian crisis later came to a head, Augustine, the greatest of the Fathers, counseled the Christians with all his strength to support the Empire as the political framework for the Christian advance. Then, with the hordes actually within the Holy City and chaos imminent, he addressed the Church to its obvious task, the conversion of the barbarians; and his *City of God* was the rallying cry for the advance. He not only presented a heavy equipment of theological ideas but also held celebrations and formalities in high regard as the means of teaching best suited to the limitations of the time. Where the Roman arms had failed to stay the inrush of these ferocious tribes, the Christian vision of its enduring city would conquer. Yet the vision alone would not be equal to the task, but must be implemented in a system of organization made dramatic with the full use of the ceremonial arts. As later the Byzantine church took over the chaos upon the fall of the Eastern Empire, actually assuming the political function and offering the only structure possible for the rebuilding, so Western Christianity was prepared—not only theologically but ceremonially—to step into the breach upon the fall of Rome.

Symbols and Ceremonies as Means of Grace

Even before the barbarian crisis the vigorous Church was pushing its way in a missionary movement, utilizing the framework of empire; and by A.D. 314 it had planted a colony in Britain, relying as much upon the persuasions of rite and ceremony as upon the pure idea. In A.D. 432 St. Patrick carried the gospel to Ireland, and within the next century and a half Pope Gregory dispatched Augustine of England on his mission of consolidating the gains and carrying the Christian belief and culture to the tribes not yet won. This great chief of missionaries wrote Augustine when he and his companions shrank before the rumors of barbarian ferocity: "Go on, in God's name! The greater your hardships the greater your crown. May the grace of almighty God protect you, and give me to see the fruit of your labor in the heavenly country! If I cannot share your toil, I shall yet share the harvest, for God knows that it is not good will that is wanting."

The conversion of King Ethelbert in A.D. 597 was one of the rewards of this heroic advance.

While it must be admitted that much of the early Chris-

tian advance relied upon the force of arms, the missionary
zeal of Gregory held to New Testament purity. We recall
the beautiful story of the pope in the slave market. Inquiring
after the Angles held in bonds, he called them "angels," and
then proceeded to win them to Christ at great hazard, using
as one of the chief means of conversion and as carrier of the
saving truth the accepted rites and customs of the Church.
Christianity was not to become primarily a system of thought
until the Schoolmen recast it in terms of Greece. During the
centuries of its conquest over Britain and the tribes of the
rough northlands, it won its way mainly by symbolism and
ceremony, whereas intellectual means would probably have
failed.

The Missionary Spread

The settlement of the Easter question was of tremendous
importance to Christianity and to the unity of the Church
in the new lands. The conversion of England is only one illustration of this. The early Christian colonies in the islands
had undergone varying fortunes. The "nations" called Picts,
Scots, Angles, Britons, Saxons, and so forth, were semi-
barbarous tribes as yet under sway of Woden and Thor. In
their conversion the ceremonial factor was of far greater
weight than the ideational. The Venerable Bede, writing of
this period early in the eighth century, gives a very large
place to ceremony, especially to that of Easter, as instrumental in the conversion of these barbarians. Also, within
the British Church, the old controversy continued long after
the decision at Nicaea, and its debate turned not only upon
questions of proper calculation but upon associated theological concerns, and thus became the vehicle for the spread
of Christian teaching. King Oswy in A.D. 652, called a meeting of the proponents of each side, and Wilfrid's speech won
the day in favor of the catholic decision. Shortly thereafter
Abbott John brought the full Church Year to England and
instructed the new converts in its every detail exactly as ob-

served at St. Peter's. The Synod of Whitby in A.D. 664 finally settled the Easter question for England. The saints' days,

too, played a large part. "The spectacle of holy lives," Bede wrote, "converted the English folk."

It must be admitted that Christianity in gaining power through official establishment lost spiritually. Now gaining the upper hand, it sometimes persecuted as much as it had been persecuted; and its shameful record in this regard gave Gibbon one of his main motifs in *The Decline and Fall of the Roman Empire.* Yet one would hardly be able to imagine the chaos that might have followed the collapse of the pagan religion after Constantine had there not been ready at hand, both as a faith and a culture, the vigorous new religion of the Christians. And it would be hard also to imagine how

Christianity without its system of ceremonial observances, rites, and liturgies could have served in the breach.

New Idolatry for Old

The conflict between Christianity and barbarism is not so much a theological debate as a warfare between God and the gods. Even as the ancient Hebrews promoted their Lord among alien faiths by showing his power to bring fire and dew at will, so the Christians evangelized the barbarians for Christ, appealing to the native credulity of the folk and answering their natural desire for miracles with The Miracle. It was not a simple task to be accomplished in a trice and by single conversions. An old legend had it that if, in those early days, one would look through the elbow of a witch akimbo, he could see the old gods; and "their power was strong in the land." Sacramental and ceremonial conversions were not total conversions of will and motive involving the instant redemption of personality to ethical religion. The old gods were powerful in the land—and in the hearts even of the converted. King Redwald, converted to Christianity, built a temple to Christ in which he also erected an altar where, in time of need, he could sacrifice to the old gods.

The conversion of Redwald, and of countless other kings and common folk, was effected more through the rite of baptism, the celebration of Easter, the worship songs of Christmastide, and the legends of the saints, than by reasoned syllogism or ethical rebirth. And while the same means of edification brought these masses gradually and painfully into fuller acceptance of Christian truth, it is not surprising that the first offering to barbarism often took the form of a christianized idolatry to replace the old gods and images. Folk but recently removed from idols might find the Christian's invisible God remote; so the barbarian heroism and heroic ideals were confronted with a convincing courage of a higher order, that of the saints and martyrs around whom there had grown an accumulation of legend.

Credulous Worship of Saints and Mary

The superstition and credulity of the masses was a fertile field for religious exploitation; and we must confess the willingness of the Christians sometimes to be satisfied with acceptance of the outward ceremony and the reception of the new culture as another idolatry, perhaps more attractive than the old. The victory period of Christianity brought a renewed interest in the martyrs and in Mary the mother of Jesus, and legend conferred a growing sanctity and power upon the great personalities of the Church. A sanguine belief in the miraculous was ready to receive any extravagance, and the gathering list of saints became the more venerable as fantastic stories about them accumulated. Prayers to the saints were in use, it being supposed they could be counted on for a mediatorial sympathy for ordinary folk. In the Nestorian controversy Mary was given the title "Mother of God," though Nestorius opposed the proposal on grounds of Christ's two natures, only one, the human, being born of Mary. The Council of Ephesus, however, accepted this title in A.D. 431, and a cluster of "Mary" days came to be added to the calendar. Irenaeus had called her the "Second Eve," and her exceptional nature was later claimed in the title "Blessed Virgin Mary." In the growth of days honoring her is seen the tendency to push back divinity to ever earlier beginnings. We saw that Epiphany placed the origin of Christ's divinity at the Baptism and that Christmas put it back at the Incarnation. The Mary celebrations signified that the divinity of Christ began in his mother's special appointment and in the virgin character of her motherhood. The Feast of the Annuncation, established by Emperor Maurice in A.D. 600, pushes the divine significance back to the angelic announcement that Mary was to become the mother of the Messiah. The Immaculate Conception, a much later introduction, having been established by Pope Pius IX in 1854, placed it at Mary's own "sinless conception." And the St. Anne observation, begun by Justianian in A.D. 533, carried it even to the grandmother of Jesus.

Surpassing reasonable commemoration, this tendency soon became a Mariology which, together with the martyrology, offered what Harnack called "a religion of the second rank." In the other direction, Mary was honored in the Feast of the Assumption, fostered by Gregory of Tours in the sixth century and based on the unbiblical tradition that Mary was bodily taken up to heaven without suffering death. In these celebrations there was a strong appeal to the love of the miraculous which is the mark of superstitious populations.

The full list of Mary days at present is:

Jan. 23 Feast of the Espousal, celebrating the marriage of Mary
Feb. 2 Feast of the Purification, or Candlemas, based on the Jewish custom of purification after childbirth
Feb. 27 St. Gabriel of the Sorrowful Mother
Mar. 25 The Annunciation to the Blessed Virgin Mary
July 26 St. Anne's Day, honoring the mother of Mary
Aug. 15 Assumption of the Blessed Virgin Mary
Sept. 8 The Nativity of the Blessed Virgin Mary, honoring the birth of Mary
September: Sunday within the octave of September 8, Festival of the Holy Name of Mary.
September: Third Sunday, Feast of the Seven Dolors of the Blessed Virgin Mary, a minor service in memory of Mary's griefs (also observed Friday in Passion Week)

October: Some Sunday, Feast of the Maternity of the Blessed Virgin
Mary, honoring the doctrine of the virgin birth (distinct from
that of the "immaculate conception")

Oct. 7   The Most Holy Rosary of the Blessed Virgin Mary

Dec. 8   The Feast of the Immaculate Conception of the Blessed
Virgin Mary

The tendency to credulity was partly checked in the rising
monastic orders and the great ascetic saints who were determined to keep the faith pure to its inner reality and to make
their lives examples of genuine holiness. Benedict in the sixth
century has been considered the father of this movement,
although many monks had preceded him during the two
hundred years since Anthony departed for his cave in the
desert and Simeon Stylites sat on his pillar. The growth of
asceticism was from the excessive individualism of these
early solitudinarians toward the group discipline seen at
its best in Benedict's order. Benedict was not the first to
bring separate monks together for mutual life. Pachomius
moved in the direction of the cloistered group; Basil in the
fourth century sought a *via media* between the hermit life
and the secular and, though thinking of the move as a com-
promise of solitary purity, found the social implication of
the Christian life as an accidental by-product. Cassian on
the southern coast of Gaul in the fifth century also followed
the group way. Benedict, profiting by these experiences,
gathered an order about him, placing them under the rule
of poverty, chastity, and obedience which became the pattern
of the later monastic rules under which countless devotees
have shaped their lives. Far from contending against the
ceremonial program of the Church, this movement advanced
it to a new height of liturgical rigor. While still encouraging
many of the superstitions, these leaders held them in a true
spirit of simple holiness, and at their best required a life of
good deeds. The need for constant reiteration is the basis
of the breviary and missal, which guide the devoted not only

in the recurring observances of holy days but through the whole liturgical week and the eight holy offices of every single day.

The saints' roll steadily grew, and the popularity of the martyrs gave an ever-wider range to the "religion of the second rank." While, as we have seen, this interest prevailed in the Church from earliest times, it was late before official sanction was given in the form of an All Saints' Day, established by Boniface IV in the seventh century, following the lead of the East. The All Saints' Day of the Eastern Church had been observed the first Sunday after Pentecost, but the day of the West was November 1. The idea was extended in All Souls' Day, begun in the ninth and established in the tenth century on November 2, upon which day not only the celebrated personalities of the Church but the entire company of the departed faithful, including the most obscure, were memorialized. Prayers were offered, not only *for* the dead, but *to* them, and masses for the departed came into vogue. Cyprian's letters show that these customs obtained as early as the third century. By the eighth the excesses were so pronounced as to call for a declaration against the worship of saints, issued by the Council of Nicea of A.D. 787.

An imposing literature has grown from this interest in the saints. *Acta Martyrum,* before the fourth century, and *Acta Sanctorum,* after the fourth century, describe the fes-

tivals already being observed. The list by the time of Bede had grown to vast proportions,,and one work of that famous writer is *Bede's Metrical Martyrology*. Many local lists had appeared under the general branch of ecclesiastical writing called hagiology. It was not until the tenth century that, in keeping with the hierarchical idea, the saints began to be canonized, the first official elevation being that of Ulrich of Augsburg by Pope John XV. Thereafter the vogue of collecting saints reached amazing proportions. *Legenda Aurea* was a twelfth-century work; Foxe's *The Book of Martyrs* covered the persecutions from A.D. 1000 to his time in the sixteenth century. *The Roman Martyrology* was written in 1583; the *Bollandist Collection* in 1643 soon reached sixty folio volumes and is not yet complete. The Rev. Alban Butler's collection in the eighteenth century, including several volumes in the unabridged editions, is a standard work today. Baring-Gould's *Lives of the Saints* is also a classic work of the present time. Numerous other collections, such as *Child's Lives of the Saints,* have appeared, all attesting the predominance of this aspect of the Christian Year from the earliest times through the Middle Ages.

Not only did every single day of the year come to have its special meaning, but almost every day offered a choice of several saints or events. The complication required rules of precedence, and finally Christian worship came to be almost as complicated as the ancient services under the Jewish ceremonial law. The "patron saint" came also into prominence, each separate place and each event having as its special protector one particular saint of the catalogue.

For all the idolatry with which the saints and Mary were adored, there is an essential soundness in the observations. Reverence for personality as a means of God's revelation is the foundation idea behind the saints' calendar. And, though the times were often marked by a gullible love of the miraculous and fantastic, there is also a considerable ethical and spiritual content to the stories, notably in the case of

St. Martin, the favorite of the ages, who gave half his cloak to a beggar, or St. Cecilia, who represented the musical heritage of the Church.

East and West

In the sixth century appear the first signs of division between the Eastern and Roman churches, pointing to a separation which is to be complete by the eleventh. In A.D. 537 Justinian dedicated the Church of St. Sophia in Constantinople, in the Byzantine style, a distinct departure from the basilicas of Rome. This style difference symbolized the deeper tensions upon the political, cultural, and religious levels. Progressively, the Greek Church would go its separate way, maintaining the Christian Year but embellishing it with its own peculiar modes and advancing ritual and music to great heights of beauty and spiritual richness. In the iconoclastic controversy it showed extreme reaction against the images, by now so common in Western worship, and limited itself to flat pictures—rather than the rounded images—as an expression of recovery from idolatry. Rome restored the icons by a later Nicene Council, A.D. 781. In the advance of the Eastern Church we see once again the persuasive power of liturgy and architectural symbolism, for the grandeur of the Church of St. Sophia and the impressiveness of its ceremonies were the deciding factor in the conversion of Vladimir I of Russia, in A.D. 988. After rejecting other religions which he had been considering as the official faith of his country, he was prevailed upon by Queen Olga, already a Christian, to consider Christianity; and he sent a delegation to visit Constantinople. Overwhelmed by their report upon the magnificence of the art and liturgy of St. Sophia, he asked, "When shall we be baptized?"

The breach between East and West was widened by the rise of a new religion of battle strength in A.D. 622. The Mohammedans began their march which was to continue through the Eastern lands, eventually to claim Palestine and the Holy City, Spain, then Constantinople itself, before being halted by Charles Martel before Tours in the eighth century.

The significance to Western Christianity of the Saracen invasion is that it presents the stern occasion for the Crusades later, in which the Christians seek to win their lands and cities back from the hands of the infidel. For the most part tragically ill-fated affairs, prompted more by excess of zeal than sound military judgment, the Crusades give a new impetus to the heroic and chivalrous element of Christianity, and from them comes an added increment of symbolism and ceremony.

We will not include in our account the development of the Eastern Church year. In its main seasons it is the same Christian Year with which we are familiar, though still related to the Jewish lunar calendar. The adaptations, which occur largely in the saints' list, would have a curious interest merely for the American Protestant. The notable emphasis in Russian sainthood is patient endurance of persecution. Since the first World War we have learned a bit more of the Greek, Russian, and other Eastern churches; and a few of their thinkers are now as familiar to American churchmen as are British or German theologians. A rich deposit of both faith and form awaits our cultivation. But for the time we concern ourselves with our own immediate tradition. East and West reached their complete separation A.D. 1054; thereafter Oriental Christianity would go along its way toward its own victories, winning the Slavic peoples as Western Christianity won the European, by the splendor of liturgy where other means might have failed.

New Additions

While there are no basic changes in the Ecclesiastical Year for a thousand years—from Constantine to the height of church power in the thirteenth century—there are certain introductions of customs from time to time. A few are worthy of mention at this point.

✳ The Rogation days came into use by the fifth century, and were made official by Bishop Mammertus of Gaul. These days—Monday, Tuesday, and Wednesday before Ascension Day—were days of special prayer in preparation for Holy Thursday. Named from the Latin verb *rogare*, "to beseech," the practice rose from a time of earthquake and terror from A.D. 460 to 470. Litanies were sung, in processionals held out of doors, in remembrance of the hazard of burning and falling buildings. These days and the Sundays preceding later came to be used as a time of praying for crops. In Elizabeth's time in England "beating the bounds" of the parish, or "perambulation," was the custom.

Sacramentaries, or formal books of religious services, appeared early, the Leonine and the Gelasian bearing the names of the popes, to whom they were attributed. Such books of public prayer accompanied the movement of religion toward formalism and regularity of usage.

Great music accompanied the development of the Church Year. Beginning with the tradition in the Psalms, Christianity improved upon the heritage from the very first. Luke's Gospel records the five great Christian hymns: Benedictus, joined with the hundredth psalm; Magnificat, with the ninety-eighth; Nunc Dimittis, with the sixty-seventh; and Ave Maria and Gloria in Excelsis. This tradition is continued through Clement of Alexandria, Ephraem the Syrian, Gregory of Nazianzus, and on into the centuries. St. Cecilia, an unauthentic but lovely character first mentioned by Venantius Fortunatus in A.D. 600, became the patron saint of music. According to the legend, she "drew an angel from the skies" with the loveliness of her playing. She was supposed to have been martyred in A.D. 230, and her tomb placed in the catacombs.

The Ember days, instituted in the Middle Ages, gave an added seasonal emphasis to the Christian Year. This is the Fast of the Four Seasons, its name being a corruption of the Latin *quatuor tempora*—"the four times." On Wednesday, Friday, and Saturday after Ash Wednesday, Pentecost, Holy Cross Day (September 14), and St. Lucy's Day (December 13), these appropriate seasonal observations are held, and the divine blessings sought upon the particular needs.

The complete weeks following the days mentioned are Ember weeks, appropriate for ordinations as well as fasting and prayer.

Swiftly after the beginning of Christianity the Church Year grew to a complete whole, its great days being extended into seasons, each joining the next, the year around. Then came additions, largely appearing in the saints' roll; and new days of significance arose from the ground of history-in-the-making, to become incorporated into the total scheme. Usages were defined, precedences established, and elaborations of minutiae developed. But the calendar with which Christianity began its conquest of European barbarism was a complete cultural unit, and this Christian Year proved one of the most effective weapons of assault upon pagan strongholds as well as of defence against disintegrating influences.

The history of the Ecclesiastical Year through the whole period of the Middle Ages is therefore one of emphases rather than of basic changes. The Church is, in this epoch, pushing forward toward the conversion of the rude hordes of Europe and their molding into an ordered and unified culture. The counterpart of the attack upon barbarism was the winning of the intellect of Europe to the Christian cause. The civilization we have come to know as that of western European culture is the result of this civilizing conquest against pagan thought and barbaric life. Both conquests were necessary to the establishment of a spiritual and cultural unity. The intellectual task of early and medieval Christianity extended from actually devising alphabets to teach the Goths to read to rationalizing a vast system of theological thought, bringing the simple Christian gospel into harmony with the predominating intellectual ideas of the ancient Greeks and converting the leaders of Rome.

In its own manner, with the Ecclesiastical Year as one of the chief offerings, Christianity moved forward to the spiritualizing and civilizing conquests which continued even during the dark times of the ninth, tenth, and eleventh centuries. The Roman advance carried the faith and culture to Bulgaria, Hungary, Bohemia, Saxony, Norway, Sweden, Poland, Denmark, and England, while the Greek Church extended Christianity to the Slavic peoples.

Chapter VII

CORRUPTIONS AND ADORNMENTS

PROTESTANT historians are apt to dwell overlong on the ignorance and superstition of these early times, forgetting the genuine beauty and spiritual validity that was mingled with the excess of credulity. This was an age of the dominance of the liturgical over the didactic—and necessarily so, considering the low literacy of the masses. The clergy, too, having been rapidly recruited from the ranks, left something wanting in general education. Protestantism is primarily a didactic expression. As such it appeared only when it was historically due. Its methods of doctrinal argumentation and evangelical exhortation almost surely would have failed in the task which the medieval Christians had before them.

The really serious corruption of liturgical practices was not in their adaptation to the superstitions which were normal to those early times but in their conversion into instruments of ecclesiastical exploitation. As the unity and authority of the Church grew and observances became universally required, the observances came to be used as sources of revenue rather than means of grace. Far-reaching historical results were to come from that perversion.

Crusades Foster Superstitions

The Crusades of the eleventh, twelfth, and thirteenth centuries gave an added impetus toward superstition, as they also promoted the spirit of chivalry. The color, movement, and pageantry of the Church Year were advanced to new heights. The dramatic sense entered into the Church as it turned its energies eastward to reclaim the holy places fallen into the hands of the infidel Saracens. In surge after surge, these reckless pilgrimages went forward, at a tremendous cost of life—of both children and men. Equipages and paraphernalia of banners, plumes, and caparisons added setting to the inherited celebrations as new customs were also promoted.

Chapels in all the churches were erected to Our Lady, and around the mother of Jesus many legends grew and caught the popular imagination and acceptance. These legends continued forming into the thirteenth century, a typical one be-

ing that the house Mary lived in at Nazareth had been carried by angels to Tersato in Dalmatia in A.D. 1291, three years later again moved through the air across the Adriatic to a wood near Recanati, and the following year to a hill at Loretto, where it could still be seen. This adoration of Mary made her almost a rival of Jesus, exerting an influence over him, as she was endowed with the powers of a goddess.

Yet new days were devoted to Jesus, emphasizing the extravagantly imaginative quality of the crusading spirit. Such observances as Corpus Christi Day, the Feast of the Sacred Heart, the Invention of the Cross, the Feast of the

Precious Blood, and Holy Cross Day were added to the celebrations of biblical origin. This emphasis upon aspects of Christianity's central figure continued to a full comple-

ment of days honoring Jesus. The present list includes the following:

Jan. 1   The Circumcision of our Lord Jesus Christ

Jan. 6   The Epiphany

Feb. 2   The Presentation of Christ in the Temple

May 3   The Invention of the Cross

July: First Sunday, Feast of the Most Precious Blood

Aug. 6   The Transfiguration

August: Last Sunday in August or October, Festival of Christ the King

Sept. 14   Exaltation of the Holy Cross, or Holy Cross Day

Dec. 16   *O Sapientia* (meaning "O Wisdom!"), a service of praise to Christ

Dec. 24   Feast of the Nativity

These days are in addition to the Sundays devoted to aspects of the life of Christ.

126

Relics, which had been held in high regard since the second century, were at a premium during this prolonged extravaganza of the period of the Crusades. They were either found or invented, and not infrequently stolen—for such a theft was not considered a sin. From the eighth century, canon law required the installation of relics at the dedication of all chapels and churches; the means by which they were secured were unimportant. These articles were endowed with all manner of magical virtues.

The air was filled with demons seeking the destruction of the Christian, and with angels to whom he could appeal for exorcising aid. St. Michael's and All Angels' Day, of uncertain origin, is emphasized in this period, harking back to an early legend and embellishing it in the revival.

The Ecclesiastical Year Mothers Literature and Drama

But it was also during this period, and no doubt partly because of the general spirit described above, that the Church Year became the mother of literature and drama. The ancient drama of Greece had suffered total eclipse, perishing, so far as European Christians were concerned, under the condemnations of the Church Fathers and the popes. It would not make its appearance again until the Renaissance. But under the spell of the Crusades three distinct types of theatricals developed: the mysteries, the moralities, and the miracle plays. The mystery plays were originally scenic dioramas mainly from the scenes of the trial and death of our Lord. The morality plays were allegorical presentations of the virtues and vices, of the type of *Everyman,* revived in our time, and *Everywoman,* patterned after it. The miracle plays presented incidents in the lives of the saints.

The ritual of the Church had a dramatic character of its own, with stately processionals and antiphonal singing. And the great festivals of the Christian Year offered audience and public psychology for the presentation of these new dramatic offerings. Their purpose was to teach, and the plays were presented originally by the priests. After Innocent III forbade the clergy to act in them, the laity took them up, corrupting them somewhat from their original purpose and turning them to coarse though good-natured travesty and comics at the expense of the clergy. One instance is the Feast of the Ass, combining the themes of Balaam's ass and Jesus' entry into Jerusalem in the humorous vein. The tendency to corruption continued, as illustrated in the Feast of Fools of the fifteenth century, a Christianized version of Saturnalia, in which the Mass is burlesqued. The line of corruption leads into the Black Mass, reaching the very depth of degradation among the decadent sophisticates of nineteenth-century Europe. This parody on the Eucharist, in which the elements are offered to his Satanic Majesty to the accompaniment of orgies, is described in the novels of J. K. Huysmans. It represents the extreme conclusion of the corruptions of Christian sanctities.

But the Elizabethan drama and plays of the modern stage come down to us in a straight line from these medieval

miracle plays; and from the mysteries comes the Passion Play, produced since the seventeenth century in the Upper Bavarian village of Oberammergau, together with modern religious pageantry.

In this time, too, the Church continued producing its great hymns, adding to the established celebrations magnificent choirs and carrying the culture of the Church still further into the popular ways. In such services as *O Sapientia,* drawn from eight greater anthems of Advent, beginning "O Sovereign Wisdom," liturgy reproduces itself by combination of earlier elements.

And in this time Dante Alighieri wrote the first great Christian dramatic poem, *The Divine Comedy,* a whole universe in itself, reflecting the pageantry of the Christian Era in the cosmic setting of man's ancient struggle as salvation joins issue with death.

The Decisive Century

The thirteenth century is the climax of the Middle Ages. Along with the spread of Christianity through liturgy, the intellectual tradition of the Church was accumulating, coming to its most complete expression in the Scholastics, of whom Thomas Aquinas was chief. In his work the sum total of things was reduced to an order in which, rank on rank, all the vocations and institutions of the world were held in hierarchical harmony as the concrete expression of the truths of Christianity. In him didacticism reached its height, yet the intellectuality of the Scholastics found ample room within the congenial boundaries of the Church. The mind had not yet broken off into the secular learning which was soon to follow, giving not only a nonreligious, but often an antireligious tone to modern times. Indicative of the reverence of this great leader of thought toward the liturgical side of religion, Thomas Aquinas left an entire office for the Feast of Corpus Christi, which had recently been instituted as a day of special remembrance of the Eucharist; and his sermons on stated days of the Church Year are a happy supplement to his extended writings on truth.

The importance of medieval scholarship depends to a

large degree upon whether one's point of view is essentially Catholic or Protestant.

To Henry Wadsworth Longfellow the vast system of medieval thought, erected by the toil of the Schoolmen, resembled the pyramids of Egypt, and the labor that went into its making, a slave labor more ignominius than that of Egypt, because "it was voluntary rather than involuntary, and of the mind rather than of the body." This rather typical Protestant estimate of the Middle Ages is not without justification.

But the Catholic historian Walsh finds sufficient evidence for his title *The Thirteenth, Greatest of Centuries.* The popes, through long quarrels with the kings of Europe, had established themselves supreme in power, with the rulers as vassals under them. The Ecclesiastical Year had reached its full height of elaboration and embellishment. Not only had the intellectual work of the Schoolmen arrived at the point of maximum elaboration, but the great university system of Europe was established, with the founding of seats of learning still in the fore in the intellectual life of the world: Oxford in England, and the universities of Paris, Padua, Bologna, and Salerno. The medieval educational system presented three main branches of study: theology, "queen of sciences"; medicine; and the law. Cathedral building had reached its highest stage of grandeur, with Gothic superseding the Romanesque. Notre Dame, begun in A.D. 1152, and the restoration of Chartres, completed in 1260, reflect in their names the popularity of Our Lady. Monasticism achieved its finest expression in Bernard of Cluny, and devoted itself not only to private holiness but to teaching the masses the rudiments of learning. The great orders of the Church were on the march—the Franciscans emphasizing the humble works of charity; the Dominicans majoring on the preaching mission; and the militant orders, such as the Templars, brought into being by the Crusades and sponsored by Bernard of Clairvaux. The Dark Ages were behind; the Church looked forward to its perpetual reign.

But, meantime, the inner corruption that always accompanies power was gathering. Here and there a sign was given, as in the "heresies" of the Cathari and the Waldenses, a sign of impending change. That the warning voices were first ignored and later persecuted was another indication of the blindness of power. That they were raised at all was a prophecy of the cataclysmic break of a new righteousness upon the old world.

Clericos Laicos

The close of this epoch of the development of the Church Year may be marked with the announcement by Pope Boniface VIII, in A.D. 1296, of the doctrine of *clericos laicos,* which set forth the complete separation between clergy and people, with full tax exemptions demanded for the Church and churchmen. We have seen that the idea of separation is basic in the growth of a new religion, that there must be a distinction between the sacred and the profane. From the third century there was distinction between clergy and laity. But it makes a difference whether men are separated from the common ranks for holiness and service or for privilege and gain. For we have also noted that self-seeking separation is as disparaging to true faith as it is damaging to the secular life. The idea of genuine holiness is then perverted into one of special privilege for an ecclesiastical group. Discussions are now to turn on such trivial matters as the proper vestments and tonsures of the clergy, and whether they should marry!

Ceremony, creed, dogmas, and now a doctrine of a specially *privileged,* rather than a specially *obligated* class, had come to enclose religion in a self-contained compartment, even while its outward culture was claiming an entire civilization. And the ancient rites and celebrations of the Church were turned into instruments of exploitation. Conditions were well advanced which would make necessary that men of the world should assert their claims and men of faith should recover their sense of obligation to the common life as religion once more permeated the cultural order.

We will see the story of the Renaissance and Reformation as reflected in the history of the Ecclesiastical Year.

Chapter VIII

AWAKENING AND REFORM

THE typical attitude of modern Protestantism toward the ceremonial side of religion is a by-product of the Renaissance and the Reformation. Whole libraries have been written on the differences and relationships between these movements, and we must remind ourselves that our purpose is limited; we are interested in the fortunes of the Christian Year during the decline of the papal power and the rise of the libertarian movements.

Renaissance and Reformation

For our purpose, the Renaissance begins with the revival of classic learning in Italy and includes the entire enterprise of secular learning, discovery, and artistic creation which broke over Europe like a daybreak and continued its enlightening influence through the Elizabethan period in England, and into the revolutionary philosophies of the modern age. It is secular and humanistic in its temper, in sharp distinction to the sanctities and supernaturalism of the Middle Ages.

The Reformation is connected with this movement, but not identical with it. The essential Reformation issue was that of merit versus grace, the same as that met by Paul when, rebelling against the intricacies of the Jewish ceremonial law, he declared for the liberty of the gospel, as a thing given and not earned. The Catholic doctrine not only had advanced the idea of human merit in the faithful observances of the formal obligations but had supported it with dogma which, by the end of our last period, had claimed for the Church a monopoly of salvation. The theory of indulgences joined to that of merit gave the Church an

133

ingenious device for raising vast revenues. The Pauline idea of salvation as the free gift of God's grace, accepted by an act of faith, had given way to one of salvation as the prerogative of the institutional Church, defined by that Church in terms of observations and rites, for the neglect of which the devoted could find forgiveness for a fee. The attack upon this system was both moral and didactic; Protestantism was a "protest" against the excessive corruptions which had entered the Church along with power, and an attack upon the dogmatic devices which supported the corruption.

Neither of these related movements is an assault upon the principle of ceremonial observations per se so much as a challenge against the intellectual, moral, and spiritual abuses of the ceremonies. The Christian Year was to be modified profoundly in its meaning, and to a great extent also in its structure, but it was destined to survive even the most pronounced antiliturgical onslaughts, remaining, on the whole, the accepted frame for the culture forms of modern Christianity as it was for the earliest.

Shadows of Coming Events

We have seen the signs of the coming change as far back as the Albigensian and Waldensian "heresies" of the twelfth

century. These movements represented a return to gospel piety and simplicity. They are typical of a number of antisacerdotal movements, which, though they had a common objective in limiting the papal power, differed in their approaches and in their ultimate purposes far enough sometimes to persecute one another. John Wycliffe, not originally rejecting the idea of the Papacy, was finally stirred to indignation by rival factions supporting two popes, one at Rome, the other in "Babylonian captivity" at Avignon, and declared, "The very idea of the Papacy is poison." John Huss in Bohemia met the Schoolmen's neglect of the

Bible with preaching in the common tongue, preparing the way for men like William Tyndale in England who translated the Scriptures into the vernacular. Zwingli united criticism of the sacramental theory of Rome with energetic social reform. Savonarola represented those who, while remaining within the mother Church, were willing to offer life to bring it to a return to the purity of Christ. Literature was coming to be a vehicle for the critical attitude. *The Vision of Piers Plowman,* by some monk of Malvern, and the *Canterbury Tales* of Geoffrey Chaucer, though marked with high reverence for the medieval world of faith and a gentleness entirely absent from the secular humanists, provoked many laughs at the expense of the priests and showed at attitude of restrained criticism toward the current practices of religion.

This tendency is far more pronounced in the secular Italian humanists Petrarch and Boccaccio, who, boldly declaring their freedom from scholastic restraints and papal denunciations, revived the old plays of Greece and invented tales whose points were always thrust toward the clergy.

The fall of Constantinople in A.D. 1453 began an influx of exile scholars into Rome; and the Renaissance was on in full, attacking the medieval system particularly at the point of its restrictions upon the free search of the mind and the attempted absorption of all scholarship in the dogmatic system. The arts, sciences, discovery, travel—all were stimulated to a high degree. This major movement found expression on its religious side in the Reformation and associated movements.

Also within the Church there were those—such as Thomas à Kempis and Catherine of Siena—who, like Francis of Assisi before, represented the saintly ideal. They offered no basic criticism of the Church but rather, accepting its authority, attempted to bring their own lives into keeping with its purest meanings. But the Church as a vast institution of power not only ignored the warning voices but, rather than conform itself to the rising demand for reform, organized the Inquisition to bulwark its failing power, with that instrument of persecution writing one of the blackest chapters in the history of Christianity.

But nothing could stay the gathering forces which, political as well as theological, religious, and literary, were combining to make an epochal shift into a new era of human thought and religion. Martin Luther, nailing his Ninety-five Theses to the door of Wittenberg Cathedral in A.D. 1517, represents that defiance of spirit to which European Christianity had been brought by a very excess of papal abuses over a series of several centuries.

Faith and Merit

The Reformation, as we have seen, was essentially the assertion of the doctrine of justification by faith through grace as against the Romanist idea of merit in ceremonial good works. The point of interest to our discussion is, however, that it did not challenge entirely the thought of an ecclesiastical year. As a matter of fact, the largest part of Protestantism still observes the classic Church Year. Lutheran and Reformed churches, Anglicans, and other Protestant branches, throughout the controversy maintained the classic frame of observations still used at St. Peter's in Rome and St. Sophia's in Constantinople. The vast majority of Christians the world over still put this Ecclesiastical Year to full use, substantially as it was in operation before the first Nicene Council.

Continental Reform Within the Ceremonial Practices

The Reformation revolted not against ecclesiastical observances as such but against their abuse under the doctrine of merit. The effort toward modification of the Church Year was a logical result of the main Protestant tendencies. These were: (1) a break with the medieval spirit; (2) a reemphasis upon the Bible, which had been neglected by the Schoolmen and finally forbidden to the masses in A.D. 1229, after the "heresies" noted above; and (3) the demand for translation of religious literature and services into vernacular tongues, this resort to the people's speech affecting the public services, including preaching. The break was more radical among the Swiss and Puritans. "Elsewhere," Fisher wrote, "Protestantism retained connection with its immediate past, and modified with latitude, each particular or national culture being free to abolish or alter."

The humanistic spirit of the Italian Renaissance was matched across the Alps with an emphasis upon man, though in the religious rather than the secular mode. This emphasis, including a distrust of the supernatural, resulted in a rejection of the medieval veneration of the Virgin and the saints, with radical revisions in the saints' list and, in certain instances, its abolition entire, except for the apostles who were first called martyrs in the Reformation period.

It is only in the English dissenting tradition that the revolutionary feeling of the Reformation was turned against the whole idea of an ecclesiastical year. Here it was a return to the Bible in the full sense of accepting only the celebrations authorized in the New Testament. This, of course, limited the Dissenters to a recognition of the Sunday worship.

137

The Lutheran and Anglican churches contented themselves with revisions—abolishing certain observations and establishing others, but retaining the total framework of the Christian Year. It is in the dissenting tradition that we find the real assault upon the very principle of observing "times and places."

Luther

Like most of the great reformers, Luther had no thought of organizing a movement outside the mother Church, but felt that he was standing for a purified Catholic Christianity and that his criticisms were against the corrupt departures from the tradition as given in the New Testament and conserved by the ancient Fathers. Theologically he was in line of succession with Paul and Augustine. He early came to

detect the usurpations of the papacy, fostered by dogmatic rationalizations of the meaning of the sacraments, especially in the light of the monetary corruptions. Early in the fourteenth century Pope John XXII was raising money through the sale of indulgences, and by A.D. 1517, the year of the Theses, the banking house of Fugger had advanced a half-million-dollar loan with commission terms of 50 per cent. Johann Tetzel was barnstorming Europe offering for sale instruments of forgiveness of sins not yet committed, and receiving untold sums for the papacy, his method of sale being that of public auction.

In Luther's treatises which provoked his excommunication, *An Address to the Christian Nobility of the German Nation* and *The Babylonian Captivity of the Church*, he attacked only the papal malpractices and those elements of the teaching of the hierarchy which tended to make religion an article of sale through ecclesiastical monopoly. He rejected the doctrine of *clericos laicos* in its entirety, together with the Church's position on transubstantiation and the ordinances requiring pilgrimages and fastings. Proclaiming the New Testament teaching of justification by faith through free grace, he pitted his force against the attempted interference with that grace by a theory of merit in ceremonial law. He was not against formalities, but rather he favored them as a means of edification while opposing their abuse as a means of revenue.

With the noted exceptions, Luther maintained the Christian Year and even prepared for his followers manuals of public worship founded on the old ritual and retaining many of the ancient forms. Confession was kept, though not as an obligatory form. Even exorcism as part of baptism was retained, and the elevation of the host at the Eucharist was dropped by the movement only after some twenty-five years. Lutheran worship centered on altar and crucifix and was embellished with instrumental and vocal music, to which the reformer added his own considerable contribution, with a range from the heroic "A Mighty Fortress" to the tender "Cradle Hymn." "All the arts," the leader said, "are not to be struck down by the gospel." He used pictures of biblical subjects. He asked: "If it is not a sin but right to have Christ's image in the heart, why should it be a sin to have it in the eyes?" The distinction he would keep was that between edification and idolatry. In this distinction he was perfectly clear, insisting upon worship "in spirit and in truth," rather than as an empty formal expression or as a token of pride in human merit. While elevating preaching to a prominent place, he did not minimize worship, saying rather, "We must be the masters of ceremonies, and not let them be the masters of us." His service books were presented as voluntary suggestions rather than as impositions of authority. Summarizing Luther's use of the Church Year, Fisher wrote:

> The Church Year was reformed, and not given up by the Lutherans. The great festivals connected with the life and work of Jesus—the Advent, Christmas, with Circumcision and Epiphany, Easter, Ascension, Whitsuntide, and the Festival of Trinity—were retained, as were also the days commemorating the apostles, the day of John the Baptist, and the feasts of the Annunciation, Purification, and Visitation of the Virgin Mary. Even the day in honor of Michael the Archangel, and that of St. Lawrence were not abolished, although from all the sacred seasons fables and superstitions were to be carefully purged away.

Luther led the way in the work of liturgical reform in 1523 and was followed by a host of men who purified and revised earlier usages, adapting them to the new purposes. They, however, did not so much original work as revisions of the services of the Latin Church, mainly their translation into the language of the people. "The whole structure of the service of the Western Church for a thousand years" was conserved. All this was the pioneer work of Protestant formal worship, and was done not only for the Lutherans but for the wider reaches of Protestantism. The Lutheran revisions were complete before the English had a prayer book, and the English work drew upon the Lutheran.

The later translation of the Lutheran order into English holds to the original Reformation purpose not to invent new forms but to decide all matters upon the common consent of prior usage. The present Common Service Book

(English) is not presented as having absolute binding authority, but rather the mind of Luther continues in the acknowledgment: "The ordering of the services of worship has been placed by Christ in the liberty of the Church, under the guidance of the Holy Ghost."

Zwingli

Zwingli, although more radical than Luther in his views on worship, did not reject ceremonies that had proved edifying even though they were not authorized in the Scripture. The bare reduction of worship modes to those prescribed in the New Testament waited for the Puritans and Dissenters of England, and the Calvinists of Geneva.

Farel and Calvin

Farel abolished the liturgy at Geneva altogether; but Calvin, recognizing the need for planned worship, prepared for Lord's Day use the Genevan liturgy, which became the model for other liturgies of Calvinist churches. Although

limiting observances to the Lord's Day, this liturgy was more elaborate than most of its successors—for instance, that of John Knox, who published the Scottish liturgy. The relative bareness of Calvin is the only noticeable exception within Continental Christianity, during these tremendous times of renaissance, reformation, and open revolt, to acceptance by all the parties of the basic need for a cultural religious calendar. Even the profound change of thought represented by the displacement of the ancient Ptolemaic with the Copernican astronomy had little effect upon the Christian Year; and Gregory's change of the Julian calendar, involving only new datings for the long-established events of ecclesiastical usage, was in the interest of accuracy rather than change.

Chapter IX

THE CHRISTIAN YEAR IN
ENGLISH PROTESTANTISM

ENGLISH Protestantism is a halfway house between the authoritarianism of Rome and the freedom of American Protestantism. Even while Christianity was growing from the earliest days through the time of Augustine of Canterbury, a democratic spirit was in evidence in England—long before King John granted the Magna Charta to the barons, laying thus the foundation for free political institutions. There was also the tendency in the Isles, as far back as St. Patrick, to remain somewhat independent of Continental Christianity. This presence of a democratic tradition, growing alongside the ecclesiastical, accounts in part for the contradictions appearing in England in Reformation times. All the issues of this period are found within this parallel development, and a main result is to be seen in the Church of England, a branch which today combines reverence for ecclesiastical tradition with theological freedom and social passion.

The English adherents of the Church of Rome are often sympathetic with the Reformation tendencies and play a large part in the Counter Reformation, which sought to continue within the mother Church the necessary changes after the main drive of the Reformation itself had been treated as a heretical movement.

Chaucer

Geoffrey Chaucer is a main link between the old and the new. John Middleton Murry finds him presenting the cultural unity of medievalism at its finest expression, the village community. His tales of parsons, nuns, peasants, and crafts-men set forth the intrinsic beauty and wholesomeness of that life even while the medievalism which created it was turning upon it to destroy it. With an impression of genuinely pious innocence Chaucer reveals some of the forces of destruction already at work; and, though a faithful son of the Church,  he informs his art with a modern—at times a "protestant"—implication. Chaucer is classic, drawing his literary materials, as he draws his very life, from "Boethius *De Consolatione,* and other books of Legends of Saints, and homilies, and morality, and devotion," for which he thanks "the Lord Jesu Christ, and his blissful mother and all the saints of heaven." He pictures the medieval community as the benevolent product of the medieval Church, the symmetrical ordering of life of neighbors living together in a unity which comes from a common sense of sin and a common recognition of divine authority, and expressing their oneness in worship and holidays. He is medieval without the medieval corruptions, and modern without acquiring modernistic irresponsibility. Murry holds that it was when the medieval Church ceased to be the Church in the true sense, and became the exploiter of the village community through the corruptions we have noted, that it destroyed its own finest expression and made way for the excesses of impious liberty which destroy our modern society.

The Monk of Malvern

The Monk of Malvern, sometimes identified as William Langland, who gave literature *The Vision of Piers Plow-man,* also reflects this period of change, and is another link between old and new. In this lengthy poem, and in the asso-ciated satirical ballads, there is a sharper note of protest than in Chaucer—protest against the corruption, immorality, and ease into which the monasteries had fallen—and an occasional sympathetic recollection of the slaughter of monks and the burning of abbeys by the enraged populace. In these allegorical cartoons the patent sins of the Church are lampooned in a manner to make the book usable by the Reformers, notably Wycliffe, who is thought to have added the "Creed of Piers Plowman" to the *Vision*. And it was popular with the masses, growing restless under exploitation. But the book was done by a monk of the Church; and he presented as the inspiration of the vision and the guide of the dreamer "Holy Church," a beautiful virgin. He was "neither a sower of sedition nor one who would be characterized by his contemporaries as a heretic." He even preached the current doctrine of obedience to rulers and refrained from attacking a single important doctrine of the Church. He was against the abuses of clergy and monks and the widespread departures of the papacy from the path of true charity and righteousness, but he entered no basic challenge against Catholic Christianity.

Indigenous Reform Movement

With men like Wycliffe, Tyndale, Ridley, Latimer, and Hooper we have the varied aspects of an indigenous English reform movement, growing within the Church and seeking at first to remain within it. In them are present the main Reformation tendencies: a return to the Bible, vernacular translations, the English tongue in public worship and preaching, and protest against financial corruptions in the Church and moral laxity in the clergy. But their protest goes hand in hand with a profoundly reverential attitude toward the continuing churchly tradition. Even the humanistic emphasis, as represented by Colet, More, and Erasmus, was no exception to the general rule that English reform at first did not attempt the total abolition of ceremonies.

The Break of Henry VIII

The revolt of Henry VIII against the Roman authority was more a personal than a religious matter, involving his desire to put away Catherine in order to marry Anne Boleyn. He was aided in this ambition by the able Thomas Cranmer, made Archbishop of Canterbury for the purpose. Henry was a Catholic in his religious views, being well versed in the scholastics. The only question he raised or settled was whether the authority of religion should be vested in the pope or in himself. The Supremacy Act of 1534, declaring the crown supreme, sealed the complete break between the Church of Rome and the Church of England. And thus the Anglican Church came into being independently of the Reformation drives, either of the Continent or at home. Those who publicly opposed Henry's usurpation were beheaded, Bishop John Fisher and Sir Thomas More being two of the most distinguished; and 376 monasteries were confiscated.

So the English Church was not Protestant, though the disturbed state of things at this time and widespread opposition to Henry gave the chance for the indigenous Protestantism which patterned itself more after Wycliffe than Luther. This movement, which we shall see more closely, became a force Henry must reckon with; and he showed a disposition to grant such concession as he could. In his Ten Articles of 1536 he granted the doctrine of justification by faith, but required also confession, absolution, and works of charity. Maintaining the orthodox line from the Bible through the historic creeds, he kept for the new Church of England the honoring of images, invocation of saints, and masses for the dead. Cranmer promoted a new translation of the Bible, drawing from Tyndale's version; and portions of the public services were turned into

146

English, while the Latin tongue remained, for the most part. The saints' list was radically revised, English leaders being entered. The Six Articles of 1539 were designed to please the Catholic element by proving the king orthodox except upon the point of his authority against that of the pope. Upon Henry's death in 1547 there were three religious parties in the realm: (1) those who wanted no considerable change in worship and who stood with the late king in rejecting foreign domination, (2) a Catholic minority who would restore power to the pope, and (3) a Protestant minority working for reform as it was known on the Continent.

In this brief background we see how the creation of the Church of England produced no great change in the long-established Ecclesiastical Year, except in the substitution of English for Continental saints and the introduction of popular nomenclature for days and seasons. It held to the main liturgical idea while rejecting Roman authority. The challenge of the very principle of observations is yet to come with the Puritans and Dissenters.

Somerset Seeks Uniformity

Somerset, protector of Henry's heir, the nine-year-old Edward VI, was Protestant in his sympathies. He granted a large degree of religious liberty, repealed the Six Articles, and ceased confiscation of church lands. In 1549 the Act of Uniformity presented the Book of Common Prayer, largely the work of Cranmer, modeled on the late medieval Sarum missal, Sacramentary of Salisbury dating from A.D. 1085 and prevalent in the thirteenth century, together with the revised Roman Breviary of 1535. Cranmer was also intimately acquainted with the Lutheran service, and was aided in his work by Bucer, Lutheran professor who had, with others, prepared the revised order of Cologne, 1543. This original English book retained many Catholic features, such as prayers for the dead, communion at burials, anointing and exorcism at baptism, and anointing of the sick. It was, indeed, too Catholic to be popular, and was followed by a series of new editions eliminating the most Roman features. The spirit of the new freedom is reflected in the preface to the revision of 1789: "It is a most invaluable part of that blessed 'liberty wherewith Christ hath made us free,' that in His worship different forms and usages may without offence be allowed, provided the substance of the faith be kept entire."

The irenic rule by then was "to seek to keep the happy mean between too much stiffness in refusing, and too much easiness in admitting variations in things once advisedly established."

After several revisions this book of Cranmer remains the guide of Anglican and American Protestant Episcopal churches. It was not widely accepted at first. Romanists disliked the changes, and Protestants thought it still too Roman. Time brought it to stable position in the English tradition, where it retains the Catholic emphasis upon unity and order, together with the Protestant demands for the test of Scripture and vernacular language.

Hugh Latimer may be quoted as representative of the group which preached with freedom within the classic tradition of the Christian Year. To them the Church Year was a guide, not a master, and their pulpit utterance sacrificed to mechanical observation nothing of prophetic freedom and spiritual reality. Latimer held to the stated days with fidelity, customarily drawing his sermons from the prescript readings. Yet one would hardly accuse this fiery, intrepid, and witty preacher of making himself a slave to the Ecclesiastical Year.

Once, before the young king and the commoners of London, he is heard in his characteristic breezy style, dismissing the daily order with a wave of his hand as he plunges into another theme that has captured his zeal. After quoting his text (not in the Prayer Book), he adds:

> This saying of Paul took me away from the Gospel that is read in the Churches this day, and it took me from the Epistle, that I would preach upon neither of them both at this time. . . . I looked upon the Gospel that is read this day but it liked me not. I looked upon the Epistle: tush, I could not away with that neither. . . . I could not frame with it. It liked me not in no sauce. Well, this saying of Paul came into my mind. . . . Then have at the root, and down with covetousness.

And so into his sermon, utterly free from any restraining influence of the Ecclesiastical Year. This freedom *within* tradition, rather than freedom *from* tradition, is a main mark of the English reform movement.

Mary Returns to Romanism

This Protestant interlude was interrupted when Mary brought Catholic ideas to the throne and, looking toward reconciliation with Rome, repealed the legislation of Edward's reign, restoring things to the last year of Henry. Restoration of papal authority was voted by Parliament in 1554, the nation was absolved of heresy, and even Henry's legislation in concession to Protestants was repealed, the Protestants fleeing to the Continent where, for the most part, they joined up with the Calvinists, since the Lutherans looked upon them with suspicion. In the purging fires that followed, seventy-five went to the stake in a year, including Master Nicholas Ridley, Hugh Latimer, and John Hooper. Cranmer, who tried to hedge both positions of an irreconcilable dilemma, was first excommunicated, then, even though making a series of recantations, executed by the woman whose mother's marriage he had pronounced invalid. On being burned at the stake at Oxford in 1556, his last gesture was his noblest: he held the hand that had signed the recantation of Protestantism in the flames until it was consumed.

Elizabeth Restores Independent Church

The Protestantism of Elizabeth was not of religious feeling but of resentment at Roman denials of her mother's marriage. The new Supremacy Act of 1559 again removed authority from the pope, and the queen became "Supreme Governor" of the Church of England, a modification of the older term "Supreme Head." The Prayer Book revision of 1559 made some gestures toward the Roman Catholics, but

under Elizabeth the Anglican episcopacy was established; its validity is still the moot point in Rome. In 1563 the Forty-two Articles were revised and became the basic statement. As at the death of Henry, Elizabeth's settlement left two opposing parties: Rome, of course; and the rising Reformers who, though having no single leadership like Luther, Zwingli, Calvin, or Knox, were to turn in the Puritan direction, rejecting the total idea of calendar usage as the empty and enslaving formalism of priestcraft. With the established religion, the classic Church Year remained, except for further revision of saints' days, and had meantime grown to popular acceptance. In Roman Catholic England today there are 250 saints' days observed, half being dedicated to royal persons. This illustrates the strong political motives in English church history.

The extreme left-wing anticeremonialists were no more acceptable to established Protestantism than to Catholicism. In Elizabeth's time the Anabaptists, Separatists, Brownists, and others, encountered the opposition of archbishops Whitgift and Bancroft, with whom the High Church movement began, the chief spokesman of which was Richard Hooker. This movement continues into present Anglicanism.

The argument of the Dissenters, as represented by Cartwright, rested upon the proposition that Christian worship was not to be confined to special times but should rather be continual. "Christians," he wrote, "are supposed to keep the feast of Easter all the days of life, not one only. For 'observing the feast of Easter' for certain days of the year doth pull out of our minds ere ever we be aware of the doctrine of the gospel, and causeth us to rest in that near consideration of our duties, for the space of a few days, which should be extended to all our life."

But the constancy called for by the reformers was more a fiction than a possibility. And the weakness of such an argument made an inviting opening in the armor of dissent. All the unsearchable riches of the gospel obviously cannot be held central in the mind all the time. Since we are creatures of time, we are compelled to observe time, and to entertain thoughts successively rather than continually. Faithful reiteration is the only constancy of which human flesh is capable. This sort of argument against Easter was an excellent argument for it, admitting its value to be so desirable as to merit extension through the year, if that were possible. And there was no reason advanced for assuming that one would be more faithful by not observing at all than he would through faithfulness to the great annual occasion of renewal of Christian hope and determination.

Hooker's *The Laws of Ecclesiastical Polity* was the classic answer to the Established Church against the Puritan extremes. A masterly work, its spirit is broad and large, even generous toward his opponents. The author seeks always to meet the crucial situation with the apparatus of reason rather than with the weapons of emotional argumentation and abuse. Being on the defensive, he is, to be sure, maneuvered into supporting the accepted ceremonial and liturgical structure entire; and the reader today feels that many pages are devoted to matters of second-rate importance and that some part of the work at least is rationalization. Yet on the whole Hooker is restrained and convincing in the central thesis, that Christian worship is not to be confined to the bare practices of the New Testament times but is privileged to add such customs as reason, convenience, and appropriateness might suggest. He does not plead authority so much as regularity and uniformity.

Answering the reform argument that the Sabbath should be the only festival, he cites the heavenly bodies as announcing daily what God hath wrought and asks whether the Church should refuse the benefits of the same lights in marking festival occasions. "These," he continues, "are the splendor and outward dignity of our religion, forcible witnesses of ancient truth, provocations to the exercise of all piety, shadows of our endless felicity in heaven, on earth everlasting records and memorials, wherein they which cannot be drawn to hearken unto what we teach, may only by looking upon what we do, in a manner read whatsoever we believe."

Wide Popular Use of the Christian Year

Everywhere through English literature is evidence of the popular acceptance of the Ecclesiastical Year. Its hold upon the people became so strong that by Elizabethan times it was part of the very folkways, a nomenclature of nicknames as well as English adaptations being in general use. "Lent" is an English word, derived from the Anglo-Saxon *lencthen* and having reference to spring. Civil events, such as terms of court, were designated according to their appearance on the church calendar, for instance, "the Lenten assizes." Shrove Tuesday took on the character of the final feast, rather than the final shriving, or penitence, before ashes; and even in England today it is a time for special dinners, with guests invited and with customs long associated with the gala occasion. The Monday before Shrove Tuesday came to be called "Collop Monday," collops being the last choice morsels of meat before the Lenten fast. The three days before Ash Wednesday came to be called "Shrovetide," and were used as a folk festival. Nicknames were given the Sundays, the nicknames sometimes being plays upon the opening words of the Collect, such as "Stir Up Sunday," the Sunday next before Advent, the name taken from the beginning prayer, "Stir up our hearts, O Lord, to make ready the way of thine only begotten Son." Again the nicknames came from the customary character of the day, such as "Low Sunday" for the Sunday following the "high" Easter Day.

Many quaint usages appear, such as the "beating of the bounds" of the parish at Rogation time. Izaak Walton has a descriptive paragraph on this custom:

He would by no means omit the customary time of procession, persuading all, both rich and poor, if they desired the preservation of love, and their parish rights and liberties, to accompany him in his *perambulation;* and most did so; in which *perambulation* he would usually express more pleasant discourse than at other times, and would then always drop some loving and facetious observations to be remembered against the next year, especially by the boys and young people; still inclining them and all his present parishioners to meekness, and mutual kindnesses, and love; because love thinks no evil, but covers a multitude of infirmities.

Another appellation for Rogation time is "gang week."

Halloween assumes the character of the prankish festival as we now know it rather than the solemn preparation for All Saints' Day, the idea being that on this night the ghosts of the dead prowl. Lammas Day, or Loaf Mass was a lesser Thanksgiving, honoring the release of Peter from prison, and celebrated with folk customs.

The literature of the period, notably Shakespeare's work reflects the extent to which the sacred times of the religious year had become part of the common life, together with the natural festivals inherited from Teutonic and Celtic ancestors. The religious seasons were no less a time of rejoicing than May Day, when the spirits of budding trees and vegetation were honored with dancing about the pole. The religious and the natural were merged together—as, for instance, in St. Valentine's Day, which was associated with the mating of birds and was considered favorable for letters and token of love. In titles and frequent reference the chief poet uses the calendar language which had become the vocabulary of the streets, and English literature ever since has done justice to the materials offered by the Christian Year as well as by the natural holidays. St. Agnes' Eve, St. Lucy's Day, St. Roch's Day, Barnaby Bright, St. John's Night, Twelfth Night, and Midsummer Night are sung in frequent rhymes and relived in the plays; and popular doggerels serve to fix the public occasions in the affections of the folk. Even the almanacs and recipe books reflect the ecclesiastical background.

In this deeply rooted sense of a mass culture, England advanced through semibarbarism to become a Christian nation; and it would be difficult to estimate the vast accretion of deeply accepted Christian sanctions and values absorbed into the common stream of English life along with its celebrations.

Reinterpretations and Latitudinarianism

Throughout the calendar history, reinterpretation of events and practices is continually in process. The question is not so simple as merely keeping or rejecting items of the calendar. Especially in a transition time, the various celebrations undergo radically different treatment of meaning as they are retained and, indeed, the whole matter of observations is brought to rest upon a different set of presuppositions. The English Church would rest upon reason, convenience, and appropriateness, the same practices which, under a more rigid authoritarianism, were established upon a basis of divine revelation. The reform movement, while itself rejecting outright many of the traditional practices, thus prompted a reinterpretation of purpose in those who retained them.

Forced Unity Under James and Charles

The reigns of James I and Charles I were marked by efforts to unify worship, partly by granting concessions to

the Puritans and partly by force. James authorized the version of the Bible of our common use today and took other steps to conciliate the demands of the Reformation. But the more extreme Puritans, rather than being satisfied with this significant gain, pressed their demands the harder for a Sunday devoid of everything except prayer and fasting. The king, impatient with their intransigence, said: "I will have only one doctrine, one discipline, one religion in substance and ceremony. . . . I will make them conform, or I will harry them out of the land, or worse." It was then that the Congregationalists fled to the Continent.

Archbishop Laud, still honored under Anglicanism for his devotion to the cause of ecclesiastical order, attempted suppression of the sects during the reign of Charles, resorting to the harshest means; and for his pains got a public reaction and ultimately, in 1645, the scaffold.

Puritanism and the "Sabbath"

The issue between the established worship order and the left-wing Christians comes to a focus in the Sabbath controversy in these two reigns.

Puritanism originally meant a purification of *worship,* rather than its later meaning of rigidity of personal morals;

and so the practices of the Christian Year on the whole became the object of discussion and attack. The first aim of the Puritans was revision rather than abolition of the Prayer Book, the guiding principles being those main stresses of Protestantism we have listed above. They were against the use of the cross in baptism, the ring in marriage, the saints' days, invocation to the saints and Mary, and copes and surplices, all on the ground that they were not authorized in Scripture. It was entirely in keeping with their literal return to Scripture that, for them, only the Sunday worship remained of the whole elaboration of customs and ceremonies of sixteen centuries.

While that quite obvious fact, that only the Lord's Day is recognized in the New Testament, did not justify the total abandonment of the historic ceremonies, the controversy did serve to re-establish the day itself in the affections and reverence of the people. The ceremonial life of the New Testament Christians was not so bare as that of the extreme reformers, having still the ancient Jewish rites in their possession. And one would have a hard time proving by the gospels that all future Christian worship was to be confined to the exact practices of the early Church and no more. The Christian liturgical development required a century or more to get a good beginning, and many centuries to grow, and we feel that the established writers had the best of the argument in claiming validity for days not prescribed in the New Testament, provided their purposes were in keeping with the spirit of Christ.

All parties were agreed that the Lord's Day was scriptural, although its proper use became the subject of heated debate and the occasion of persecutions.

The True Doctrine of the Sabbath, by the Rev. Nicholas Bownd, written in A.D. 1606, became the Puritan norm. The title itself shows how the Puritans read back into Sunday, or the Lord's Day, the Old Testament meanings which properly belong to the Jewish Sabbath. This tendency was peculiar to the English-speaking countries, and is not found even in the strictest of the Continental reformers, Luther and Calvin, nor in Knox of Scotland. Strictly speaking, this rigorous Jewish interpretation of Sunday is not a Reformation tendency but the insistence of those Reformation minorities known as the Puritans and Separatists. Although Puritan harshness is a much overdone theme, there is no doubt the Puritans went far toward converting the one day they allowed to remain in the Christian Year from its original use as a day of rejoicing to one of suppression, in so far as their power enabled them from time to time entering restrictions and prohibitions on the normal recreations of life. It became necessary for the political power to defend the common folk from encroachments on their legitimate weekend pleasures.

James issued the famous Book of Sports in 1621, designating permissible Sunday recreations; and he not only encouraged people to repair to their playgrounds following divine worship but ordered the clergy to read the Book of Sports from the pulpit. Naturally the Puritans hated the work; and they refused to obey, accepting their punishment and abiding time until they could burn the book at the execution of Charles.

The revolution following brought Cromwell to power with his policy of "tolerance." The tolerance of the Commonwealth, however, applied to the sects only, while prohibitive laws were passed against Easter observance and other calendar usages, with severe penalties; and the Blue Sunday came into its own, while, in their turn, the High Churchmen suffered martyrdom. The rigid Commonwealth "Sabbath" retained little trace of the spontaneous spiritual joy, praise, and gratitude of the day of the early Christians, even while seeking its justification in a return to the Bible. If formalism and frivolity, with its rules and precedents, had run to seed in Romanism and Anglicanism, surely the stiffness and joylessness of the Puritan decrees was an overcorrection.

Next came the Stuarts and the "great eviction" by use of the instruments of oppression known as the Act of Uniformity, the Five Mile Act, and the Conventicle Act, with rigid restrictions against public assembly of more than five in unauthorized meetings. And Bunyan, Fox, and thousands of nonconformers were sent to prison.

And so, back and forth, until the situation came to rest in the later Toleration Act which offered the *modus operandi* by which the liberal and radical sects could operate along with the established religion.

The Anglicans did not wholly reject the Jewish-Puritan idea of the Sabbath as a day of rest, but they refused to interpret rest as pious idleness and found no fault with a recreational use of the day by the working masses. One of our greatest hymns, "O Day of Rest and Gladness," is a product of the later High Church movement and of the pen of an English bishop, Christopher Wordsworth.

This controversy has a faint echo today in the mild shock Protestant laymen sometimes experience on seeing gentlemen in clericals at Sunday baseball. And a National Sunday League still exists to advocate the use of Sunday for recreation and secular education, while the Lord's Day Alliance fosters reverence for the day more in the Puritan spirit.

Dissenters and Separatists Abolish Times and Seasons

The various groups of Dissenters and Separatists went even beyond the Puritan position, and in rebelling against the Roman corruptions they tried to discard every reminder of the hated domination of the papists, seeing in every liturgical suggestion a "return to Popery." George Fox and the Friends were even "separatists" *from* the Separatists, opposing all the "priests" who took money for their hire. Fox's total reaction against the outward signs of religion is shown in his contempt for the church buildings, which he always called "steeple houses," or "mass houses," and into which he never went except to witness against the "hired priest" and the Church itself. Standing on a pew, because he scorned pulpits, he urged the people to desert the Church and follow the plain gospel way. Rejecting all "times and places," he referred, not to Easter or Christmas, but to "the time called Easter," and "the time called Christmas," while inveighing against their holiday uses. Going even beyond the

Puritans, he rejected also the Lord's Day, and would refer to it only as "the first day," it being on a par with the "second," "third," and all the rest, which he never complimented, even by their names of common usage. He not only criticized the stated celebrations as not being needed by earnest Christians but denounced them as positively harmful, cultivating, in the popular corruptions, attitudes the very opposite of those they were supposed to foster. "When the time called Christmas came," he wrote in his *Journal,* describing his boyhood, "while others were feasting and sporting themselves, I would have gone and looked out poor widows from house to house, and have given them some money."

The demands of the extremists reached a climax in the Easter and Christmas controversies, in which the issues were not merely debated in theological circles but engaged in the streets, where crowds marched and picketed churches with "No Christmas" or "No Easter" banners.

Two Centuries of Conflict

The controversy extended over two centuries, and has not yet so much been resolved as come to rest. It involved the harshest asperities and mutual persecutions as one side, then the other, gained the ascendency and managed political power. Many of the finest spirits and minds of the sixteenth and seventeenth centuries met death by burning, hanging, or beheading; as many, perhaps, being martyred for the cause of unity as for the cause of liberty.

These two centuries of controversy, in which the Christian Year had so important a stake, came not so much to a final decision as to a stalemate. Throughout, and even down to the present, the three main lines of Christianity were in evidence in England: the independent Established Church, the Roman Catholic, and the reformers. The first two, of course, retained the full use of the Ecclesiastical Year, while the last, for the most part, rejected it. Each of the contending groups left modifications upon the others. The Counter Reformation within the Catholic Church, both in England and on the Continent, to some extent absorbed the zeal of the reformers in bringing about needed purification of practice, while at the same time effort was made to check the further spread of "heresy."

The Church of England was even more profoundly affected by the modern movement. It became an English-speaking church with an English Bible, thus adopting one of the cardinal tenets of the Reformation. Through its greatest preachers and its mystic poets, the Established Church recognized and accepted the liberalizing elements of the Reformation; and while holding to the classical liturgies and ceremonies, it put into them a deeper spiritual, social, and moral meaning. And thus, as we have noted, the English expression of Christianity has been ever since a halfway house between Roman authoritarianism and Protestant libertarianism. In its American phase it incorporated the name of the Reformation, being known as the *Protestant* Episcopal Church.

The revolutionary elements had their good and bad points. They were represented at their best dignity in men like John Milton, who, while Latin secretary to Oliver Cromwell, declared in favor of the two most important people in any state, those who make it "just and holy" and those who make it "splendid and beautiful," insisting that the very stability of the state depends upon "the splendor and excellence of its public institutions." He was seeking that cooperation of Puritanism with the arts that came to its best expression in the architecture of Christopher Wren and in the high magnificence of his own *Paradise Lost*.

Stuart P. Sherman, in an essay provoked by the onslaught against Puritanism of the Mencken era in our time, appraised these prophetic men: "Under persecution and in power, on the scaffold, in war, and in the wilderness, they proved that, whatever their faults, they were animated by a passionate sincerity." The Puritans influenced the Church of England and the Church of Rome more than they were influenced by them. And now, time having overcome the sharp edge of their temper, they have accepted if not embraced many of the liturgical and ceremonial practices for which they once suffered and inflicted suffering.

Chapter X

THE CHRISTIAN YEAR IN AMERICA

FOR a hundred years prior to the Reformation, the missionary activity of the Church was suspended. Its original magnificent impulse had conquered the strongholds of pagan thought and the great areas of European barbarism. But the excessive zeal of the Crusades resulted in disillusionment, and the end of the Middle Ages manifested decay in missionary motive as in all other phases of religion. It was obvious that the next great task that lay before Christianity was the conversion of the heathen in every land, in fulfillment of the "great commission." And now, with the awakening of the Renaissance and the Reformation, a new missionary century was prepared, during which the event most significant to our study was to be the discovery and colonization of America.

Religious Motive for Colonization

This reawakening of Christianity to its characteristic spirit accompanied the general cultural ferment of the Renaissance, and the new missionary enterprise went hand in hand with the ambition for new discovery. The late fifteenth and sixteenth centuries were the time of Vasco da Gama, Bartolomé de Las Casas, Francis Xavier, Bartholomeu Dias, and Christopher Columbus. While a trading and colonizing motive is prominent in this expansion, there is not lacking a genuine religious purpose, seen in the fact that among these men are priests and missionaries and behind them certain Christian rulers, like Isabella, who give their enterprises support. The discovery of America, therefore, is not simply an occurrence of secular history but definitely a chapter in the

further extension of the Christian culture in some sense of a piece with the missionary occupations of Japan and the Congo. While it is quite beyond our present purpose to give a complete account of the religious factor in American history, it needs at least a passing emphasis, partially in protest against the recent American histories that wholly ignore that factor. It is rather an amazing discovery to find that many historians of high standing are apparently innocent of any information on this important aspect of the national life.

First Extensions by Ceremonial Religion

The new missionary awakening took place among the Catholics first. The Reformation people, including Martin Luther, entertained a strong eschatological hope; and an excessive Messianism usually paralyzes practical advance. Further, Protestant energies were occupied with consolidation of their immediate gains and the organization of churches. The Lutherans for more than a century held to this bias against missions, even denouncing Baron von Welz, who in 1664 called for the organization of an "extension society." Another reason for Roman supremacy in missionary work was the strategic position of the Church of Rome with the rulers under whom maritime activities were sponsored.

Where the Catholics went, of course, they carried the liturgical equipment with them, introducing the ecclesiastical celebrations of St. Peter's with such accommodations as were necessary to the local situation. The Jesuits by the time of the Pilgrims' landing were already suffering martyrdom for their witness and achieving success in the spread of liturgical Christianity, in Japan, China, India, Mexico, Paraguay, Canada, and among the American Indians. Also, in advance of the Puritans, the Episcopalians had occupied positions to the extent of introducing the Established Church in Virginia and Maryland.

Colonial Protestantism the Determining Culture

But those who had fled the fury of James were destined to be the carriers of the dominant Christian expression of America. Colonial Protestantism emphasized three main strains; the didactic, the evangelical, and the reformist. And each of these emphases was antiliturgical. In returning to the Bible, the Puritans had found there its great doctrines, its persuasive appeal, and its moral challenge, rather than its ancient ceremonies. They were preachers after the prophets of Israel, and teachers and evangelists after Paul. And their preoccupation with making a new society left little room for concern over the symbolisms of the old.

Reformist Suspicion of Form

It should be noted that this suspicion toward the ceremonial, however, has no necessary relationship to the chief Puritan concerns. The history with which we have been dealing offers ample evidence that the cultural practices of the Ecclesiastical Year have possibilities in all the emphases we have noted as belonging intimately to the forefathers. It had been for sixteen centuries the carrier of the great Christian doctrines, and it remained the main agency for teaching and evangelizing. Further, there is no basis for making any necessary or exclusive association of ceremonies with the episcopal and papal polities. But the association was made in the minds of the reformers, and the rites were identified with the corruptions which were the real object of attack. It was in a manner similar to the Russian situation of our time, when revolutionary rage against oppression was transferred from the corrupt Russian Orthodox Church to all religion and official atheism was established. As the Russians punished religion itself for the sins of certain ecclesiastical organization, so the Puritans punished ceremonies and liturgies, as such, for the sins committed by a church which happened to be ceremonial and liturgical.

Something of that distrust of religious formalities of "days and seasons" has persisted even to our own times, with only a very recent re-emphasis on some of the values of common observances. It was enhanced by the secular modes of thinking of the deists and other products of the Enlightenment, introduced into American life with men like Jefferson, Franklin, and Paine.

Local Celebrations and Observances Begin

It is of special interest, therefore, that our forefathers really failed in their determination to abolish "times and places." For hardly had they arrived on these shores before they began the establishment of their own simple calendar. So deeply rooted in the order of creation and the social life is the custom of time measurement and religious designations that even the men who had rejected all formalities not prescribed in Holy Writ began to devise ceremonies not biblically required. The beginning was informal, as would be expected; but the ceremonial principle was recognized in the appointment of special days for "humiliation" or "rejoicing" in times of special stress under attack or famine or in times of harvest after tribulation. Such occasions—which are frequently recorded in *Chronicles of the Pilgrim Fathers*— were the perfectly natural social expression of a people whose primary motive for colonization was religious.

The Pilgrims' Thanksgiving Day, immediately taking root in the natural feelings and experiences of the people, grew to national importance as a general civil holiday and is now incorporated into the calendars of both Anglicans and Ro-

man Catholics, with fitting collects, lessons, and hymns. In this manner the most antiliturgical branch of the Church made a lasting contribution to the most liturgical branches, even while continuing to look askance upon religious observances as such. And there is a bit of irony in the fact that these stern opponents of "appointed times" are now remembered with honor throughout Protestantism on Forefathers' Day, on the anniversary of their landing at Plymouth, December 21.

The Revolution

The American Revolution gave no aid nor comfort to liturgical Christianity as represented by the Episcopalians. They were held in suspicion as royalists; and the presence of unworthy clergy, together with their persecution of the free sects, brought them into disfavor with the forces of national independence. The doctrine of the new republic requiring the separation of church and state disestablished them in Virginia and Maryland, their strongholds. Consequently, it was

somewhat of a concession to the new liberalizing forces that upon the formation of an American church independent of the Church of England, in a series of meetings from 1785 to 1789, the word "Protestant" was incorporated into their name, which became the Protestant Episcopal Church in America.

The Classical Minority

Roman Catholicism, Episcopalianism, and Lutheranism, the three ceremonial branches of the universal Church, were to be a minority in the American situation. And, until very recently, every major movement in American religion seems to have favored the free and informal, as against the unified and ordered, expression of faith. It was natural that Congregationalists and Presbyterians occupied themselves largely with the social aspects of religion, lending their best powers to the development of the infant political order and advancing along the line of reform through the slavery period, and beyond. The Methodists, early to become a very large influence, left their Anglican heritage behind in favor of the zealous evangelism of the period of "the wilderness aflame"; and, forgetting that their founder was never pictured except in the ecclesiastical robes of the Church of England, they discarded all semblance of priestliness, cultivating the mass appeal through gospel songs and exhortations. The Baptists brought into the situation a very passion for freedom, interpreted in terms of the English dissent. Of the three hundred denominational groups which came on in turn, all were products in some degree of the English or Genevan expressions of the Reformation.

Religious Movements

English Protestantism was still producing new movements, such as the Sunday schools, the Salvation Army, and the new missionary activities, all furthering the nonceremonial interpretation of religion.

And in America movements followed one another throughout the national history, each offering some profound emphasis, but never a suggestion of rediscovery of the Christian Year until very lately. The Great Awakening, led by Edwards, Whitefield, and the Tennent brothers; the missionary movement of the beginning of the nineteenth century, when the American (Congregationalist), Presbyterian, Methodist, and Baptist boards were formed; the abolitionist movement prior to and during the Civil War; the Bible societies; the evangelistic period of the great camp meetings, as the nation trekked westward; the educational advance in the wake of evangelism, with its academies and colleges in every town of size; the era of professional revivalism; the modernist-fundamentalist controversy; and moral rearmament—all these movements and enterprises were prompted in the informal tradition. They were all great in their kind, and it is in no sense an underestimation of their enormous contributions to vital Christianity to observe that not one of these varied manifestations explored the ritualistic and ceremonial values of classic Christianity.

Even so, that stubbornness we have noted, which is a characteristic of deeply rooted folk celebrations, insured against the total extermination of observances. Easter and Christmas, for instance, for most of the Protestant sects as well as for the total civilian population, continued as high holidays. Experimental Protestantism held to these main items of the old order through no conscious reverence toward the Christian Year, as such, but rather because of the vitality of the customs and their depth of rooting in the social practice of many centuries. The Thanksgiving day begun by the Pilgrims and soon established as a civil occasion by Governor Bradford was really a revival of the old harvest tradition, whose origin is lost in antiquity. A few antiliturgical sects disposed even of these great days in their zeal for purity. But the impressive fact is the persistence of the ancient calendar usages and the continuity of observances even through the most excessive periods of religious experimentalism and subjectivism.

For all the informality of American Christianity, the nation was never given to anticlericalism or to antireligious tempers. On the contrary, religion was magnified in the common life and recognized in the institutions. The strong motivation of the colonists continued as the recognized drive of national life, and the popular sanctions were those of Bible Christianity, even after waves of new immigration made the original stock into a minority. Not even those who came under the influence of the Enlightenment gave it the accent of hostility to faith such as appeared in France; but, though modifying their religion in the direction of Deism and frequently having no membership in the orthodox churches, these men of the "Age of Reason" maintained a profound regard for religion itself.

The chaplaincy of the legislative houses; the oaths of officers, jurors, and witnesses; the slogan stamped on the coinage—all these symbolized this attitude of America toward things of divinity.

French Anticlericalism and the Antireligious Temper

By sharp contrast, the French Revolution was violently against the clergy, the Church, and religion itself. France had remained relatively insulated from the Reformation influences by the Catholic violence against the Huguenots, and consequently her medieval corruptions were left to accumulate to the point of exciting the revolutionary leaders to great fury, showing itself not only in the satanic vengeance of the people's court but in a most unnatural rejection of the total calendar of national customs. In a mania of destruction, the attempt was made to destroy, root and branch, every vestige of the hated order. Sunday was ignored in a system of "decades" to replace the week, each tenth day being a day of rest and three decades making equal months of thirty days.

Five or six extra days were added to equalize, these named "sans-culottides" for the proletariat. Four-year periods were marked off as "Franciade," symbol of the excessive nationalism of the hour. The months were renamed: *Vendémiaire, Brumaire, Frimaire, Nivôse, Pluviôse, Ventôse, Germinal, Floréal, Prairial, Messidor, Thermidor,* and *Fructidor.*

All the fasts and festivals of the classic Christian Year were thrown out bodily, together with the saints' days, which were replaced with national holidays, called "gentlemen's days," commemorating the revolutionary heroes. This excessive effort failed. From the first it was simply not accepted, even by the revolutionary masses themselves, so strong were the old social habits. New affections cannot be artificially imposed upon the folk, nor can they be persuaded by an edict from remembering what is customary as well as dear. In such matters the folk themselves are the original and final authority. As we have seen, even slight calendar reforms are often the fruition of centuries of accumulating change, and new events must prove themselves through long seasons of growing social usage before there is proper public preparedness for the official pronouncement, which is the last stage of the process rather than the first. A brief twelve years marked the life-span of this ill-advised effort, the Republican calendar having been enacted by assembly October 8, 1793, retroactively to September 22, 1792, and abolished by law December 31, 1805.

American Religious Motive in the Informal Tradition

While America was spared even so much as a show of antireligious violence in her revolutionary period, but, on the contrary, saw religious meaning in the upheaval, the attitudes and influences we have already outlined continued to work against the ordering of her religious life into a unified system of observances. The continuing emphases of the Reformation are seen in Auguste Sabatier's *Religions of Authority and the Religion of the Spirit* and Henry C. Sheldon's *Sacerdotalism in the Nineteenth Century,* one French and the other American. Both, in scholarly rather than polemic vein, express the distrust of both these national cultures toward the liturgical types of religion.

Liberal Protestantism and Ecclesiastical Usage

That distrust, with its common assumption that liturgy and celebrations necessarily militate against the vital experience, became a recurring theme of American Protestant preaching, with the stock illustrations drawn from the controversies and martyrdoms of the Puritans and Dissenters and "the Dark Ages" used as whipping boy. Dr. Lewis O. Brastow in the Yale lectures on preaching, published under the title *The Modern Pulpit* in 1906, expressed this typical Protestant suspicion with more than ordinary restraint. This quotation may be taken as the voice of liberal Protestantism on the matter of the Ecclesiastical Year:

One questions whether the dominance, not to say the tyranny, of the Christian year, with its necessary multiplication of public services, and its necessary repetition of themes and texts, may not measureably limit the effectiveness of Anglican preaching, partly by diminishing the preacher's sense of the importance of the individual sermon, or by limiting his time of preparation, or by overtaxing his homiletic inventiveness.

He perhaps overdid the theme of the low grade of Anglican preaching, painting its pulpit utterance as a drawling, liturgical monotone devoid of spiritual life, mental excitement, or moral imagination. He might have remembered such royal preachers as Hugh Latimer, Phillips Brooks, John Henry Newman, and others who preached entirely within the framework of the Church Year. At any rate it would be an oversimplification of the continuing problem of formalism to attribute all the ills of a time or of a branch of the Church to the one fact of observing the classic celebrations.

Development of New and Restoration of Old

Curiously enough, the nation which perhaps more than any other has in its religious life stressed opposition to stated occasions has accumulated during its brief history a vast number of special days, weeks, and seasons, drawn from civic and religious aspects of its life. Strictly speaking, there are no "national" holidays in the United States, the public observances being matters of common custom or of presidential or gubernatorial proclamation rather than of Federal legislative enactment. A swift review of the general categories of the celebrations surprises one with the varied interests represented and with the emphasis of the national culture revealed.

We have suggested that, despite the Dissent, the main events of the classic Christian Year remained—including, particularly, Sunday observance, Easter, and Christmas.

Later we will indicate the renewed interest which of late has revived many other parts of the calendar. Other classic concerns which are not in the traditional calendar have been introduced, such as the Festival of Christ the King, Vocation Day, Theological Seminary Day, and Week of the Ministry.

Other celebrations have come from Protestant history—such as Reformation Day, Thanksgiving, Forefathers' Day, Universal Bible Sunday—and from the regular observances that stem from the inception of the Sunday schools—such as Children's Day, Religious Education Week, Youth Sundays, and White Christmas. The Protestant missionary and evangelistic enterprises have added their quotas of appointed times—for instance, the Universal Week of Prayer; the Day of Prayer; and special days of prayer for students, for China, and so forth; Men and Missions Sunday, Missions in the Sunday Schools Day, World-wide Communion Sunday, Stewardship Day, and Decision days.

The various denominations have also instituted their own special occasions representative of the sectarian histories, their great personalities, or their group programs. And the local churches in many cases have acquired traditional customs centering on their dedication dates, loyalty drives, or other emphases important to the individual society. A few of these local traditions have been more widely received by the general church public.

The religious appreciation of personality has been expressed in observances of a growing list which might be called an American Protestant adaptation of the saints' roll. Some of the better known of the classic saints remain to bless Protestants, such as St. Francis, St. Theresa, St. Anthony, and St. Augustine. However, the mythological and miraculous are not stressed in connection with these so much as the historical and biographical. And supplementing these historic Christians, the heroes of Protestant experience and the fathers of the various denominations—such as Luther, Wesley, Calvin—are honored in the public services, as well as such national heroes as Washington, Jefferson, and Lincoln.

The national history comes in for its emphasis, illustrating how close may be the relationship between church and state in a society which believes in their functional separation. Such days as Thanksgiving, Independence Day, Bill of Rights Day, Constitution Day, Flag Day, and Memorial Day are among the stated times when the national tradition is honored by the churches. Columbus Day is both classic and national.

The widespread Protestant emphasis upon the social aspects of Christianity is recorded in an imposing list of special observances of greater or less general acceptance, such as Labor Day, Interrace Sunday, Good Will Sunday, Red Cross Day, Temperance Sunday, and Rural Life Sunday.

The family has also its healthy emphasis in the traditional Mothers' Day, now called the Festival of the Christian Home and closing Christian Family Week; Fathers' Day, Fathers' and Sons' Day, Mothers' and Daughters' Day, and the children's and youth's days already mentioned.

Other cultural and political interests are represented in Pan-American Day, Poetry Week, Book Week, Nature Sunday.

The first World War contributed to the accepted calendar Armistice Day, usually observed as a time of national penitence and commitment to world friendship. And we will reserve for later comment the stimulation of the present war effort toward special observances.

It is obvious that the Separatist effort to abolish all special "days and seasons" failed in its purpose and that the main result of the effort was to produce another national calendar which, though unplanned, reflects in a fair measure the spirit of the national culture and religion.

This brief survey is not to be understood as implying a

recommendation for the indiscriminate adoption of these various observances as a substitute for the classic Christian Year. Of all the new offerings, perhaps the majority will be discarded with time. Yet the Church Year will remain elastic in sufficient degree to admit occasional adaptations to changing times and to new insights and emphases of the ancient faith.

Chapter XI

THE PRESENT PROSPECT

THE present problem is that of the anarchism of public observances of the general and religious culture, despite certain trends in the direction of the classic Christian Year, which I shall discuss later. If on the one side there has been the danger of formalism, on the other is planlessness, which is equally dangerous.

Secularism Overwhelms the Sanctities

Every church and every minister follows some sort of calendar after a fashion. But without conscious adoption of a recognized scheme there is no protection against the multitude of days and weeks that special interests seek to foster. The planless minister and the church without a program can hardly expect otherwise than to be victimized by these secular inroads upon sacred times, and very frequently they will lend the prestige of Christian faith to some questionable cause on a day to which the centuries have assigned opposite meaning.

Frank E. Wilson pointed this warning: "Constantly the Church is under pressure to devote various Sundays to the exploitation of certain efforts in which groups of people are particularly interested."

Some of these causes are commendable social efforts which the Church might help with a simple announcement, or by inclusion in a week-night meeting. Others are entirely beyond the range of the acceptable. It is curious to look into the calendars of some of the most vigorous opponents of the idea of a stated church order, to discover some of the fantastic introductions they have made to public worship in the name of "community co-operation."

Of course commendable social efforts may expect the Church to lend aid, but this can usually be done through educational meetings or the customary channels of publicity rather than as an addendum to, or usurpation of, divine worship. It is when whole days or weeks are asked for, or even boiler-plate sermons and services are submitted, that the minister should be well enough grounded in an established program to resist with firmness.

Among the items that come to the minister's desk are countless proposals prompted by trivial sentiment or an obvious commercial motive. His surest protection against the barrage of salesmanship and propaganda is a true sense of the wisdom of the Church as a whole as to the proper use of its holy times and places. He may well be open to innovations, remembering that every item of the classic calendar was once an innovation, and yet he must maintain a sound judgment as to the appropriateness of each new suggestion. Familiarity with the classic order of the year need not bind him to its mechanical use.

The present war, with its period of preparation, has promoted a number of special days, originating mostly with private groups, but to some extent by proclamation of mayors or governors. Most of the requests for such days are based upon ignorance of the Church Year and advanced by persons who seem neither to know nor to care that they are proposing radical amendments of a calendar long established in religious usage. When they are made to ministers equally ignorant of the Christian Year, they are often adopted with thanks for a welcome suggestion to an otherwise unoccupied mind and program.

At such points the whole problem of the relation of religion to government is seen in sharp focus. The attitude of the churches indicated by negative responses is not a display of antipatriotic feeling. The established practices of all branches of Christendom recognize the governmental concern, and several appropriate occasions through the year are devoted to celebrating these national values consonant with the universalism of Christianity. Further, the sensitivity of the churches to irresponsible suggestions comes from a sound instinct for the preservation of religious liberties. Obviously there are matters in which religion and government find themselves in co-operative relationship; and quite as obviously, in the modern world as well as the ancient, there are other matters in which church and state must mutually recognize areas of independence. The point that here concerns us is the necessary independence of the Church in making its own decisions, upon a basis of its own presuppositions, on all matters having to do with pulpit and altar.

Some of the gratuitous offerings are not only inconvenient and inappropriate but actually contrary to Christianity.

Planless Anarchism

A planless anarchism is no defense against such attempted encroachments. Nor does it protect a preacher against his own inventions, extravagances, and enthusiasms. Rare would be the preacher who, without an objective order to guide him, could avoid the hobbies of emphasis which tempt us all. The man may be an extreme example who embarked on a series of thirty-five sermons on Dante, only to find himself without a pulpit before he was well along on his task. Most of us are not so bad; but we all fall short of the wholeness of the gospel entrusted to us and will, despite our best efforts, fall into ringing the changes on a private inspiration.

The question is not whether we shall have a calendar. Who is without his little black book? As individuals and as a national religious culture, we have a calendar of a sort, and any year end will show that we have in some fashion observed a certain list of interests. The question is whether our own scheme, made piece-meal day by day and week by week, under pressure from the secular order, and finally determined by our own subjective tastes, is better than one guided by the long growth of the Christian ages.

In its determination to overcome the medieval abuse of the principle of separation between sacred and profane, Protestantism moved toward their union, with the intention of redeeming the profane by making all life sacred. But the end result of that overemphasis was that the secular rose up to overwhelm divinity, and nothing is so deeply needed as a revived sense of the separation. This achievement in life and thought is basic to any revival of religion. And since the deeper things of the spirit are symbolized in the outward disciplines, the disorganization of the Christian Year reflects the secularization of life and thought which is religion's greatest challenge today. The altars of faith have been profaned, the sacred times violated. A self-examining church must assess much of the blame upon its exaggerated suspicion of all ceremonies and its disregard of their importance. It is an interesting commentary on how poorly American Protestantism has instructed the people in the religious significances of observances, that few persons know the original meaning of Halloween. An "inquiring reporter" recently raised the question whether the day should be abolished on account of the destructions of pranksters. Of the whole column of answers, only one betrayed any knowledge of the original meaning of the day as the Eve of All Saints' Day. All justified continuance of the "spook night" on the ground that young people are entitled to their fun; and one ventured a social interpretation, arguing that if the pranksters destroyed fences it would perhaps make better neighbors, borrowing the idea from a poem of Robert Frost.

Influences for the Revival of the Christian Year

The influences that bring the Church Year back to Protestant consciousness are: (1) the revived interest in worship as the highest communal art; (2) the rapid growth of the ecumenical consciousness, with its emphasis on the nature of the Church, its expanded sympathy and understanding between the various branches, and its recognition of the practical necessity for unity; (3) the emphasis upon planning, with the year as the unit for preaching programs and church activities; and (4) the deepening devotional search in crisis times, leading many to a recovery of the classic means.

We seem ready now for a Protestant-modified, somewhat Americanized, version of the classic Christian Year. Indeed that rather well describes the present practice of American churches. Denominational centers are rapidly furthering the idea of planning church programs with an eye to seasonal appropriateness; and they have for many years been issuing aids for Advent, Lent, Pentecost, and so forth. The various "interests" of the denominations—missions, social action, education, stewardship, evangelism—are given assigned places upon the calendar. The Federal Council of Churches distributes excellent materials—in the form of services, syllabuses, and bibliographies—for educational, social, or worship days, and through its departments has originated new celebrations. Separate organizations with specialized interests have promoted their particular days into places of prominence on the calendar, for instance, the Universal Bible Sunday, and Heroes of Peace Day.

Some direct attention has been given to the Christian Year in such books as Howard Chandler Robbins' *Preaching the Gospel,* George P. Hedley's *A Christian Year,* and *The Ministers' Annual,* edited by Joseph McCray Ramsey for the *Expositor and Homiletic Review.* These, and many other books, pamphlets, and periodicals follow the general scheme of the Christian Year, though making no study of its history or restatement of its motifs.

These trends in Protestantism of late years have sent scholars to the sources of liturgy and symbolism. And a renewed devotional life among Christians has resulted in a wide use of external "helps" after the pattern of *The Upper Room* and *Today,* all of which follow the classic patterns.

There has been also a pronounced liturgical revival in the liturgical churches themselves, a full account of which lies

181

beyond the scope of this work. The movement among Catholics was heralded by the papal encyclical, *The Mystical Body,* by Pope Pius XII; and a large literature has followed in the Roman and Anglican churches. The primary emphasis of this movement is upon the essential nature of the Church universal. To this end the meaning of liturgy and the symbolic arts has been re-explored. A strong social and ethical note accompanies that of worship. The revival of liturgical worship, far from being the escape it is sometimes described as being, finds its chief support from those sections of the Church most deeply involved in social action.

This neoclassicism finds a parallel in the Tractarian, or Oxford, movement in England in the middle of the past century and may be seen as a delayed response to the challenge of Protestantism's excess of individualism and subjectivism. The English debate revived about 1830 with a sermon from John Henry Newman. The Christian Year was done into poetry by John Keble, and a flood of pamphlets came from the distinguished pens of Manning, Pusey, and others of the High Church party. It was a reaction against such secularization and disorganization of the worshiping community as we have indicated above. In them the modern mind returns in reverence to tradition, while yet remaining modern in many respects. John Henry Newman, who was to follow through the Oxford movement into the Roman fold, shows the mark of the modern in his justification of saints' days. Entirely free from the superstitious credulity of the Middle Ages, he rests the institution of saints' days upon the value of personality as a channel of revelation, a very modern idea. On the particular benefits of these observances, he says: "So much of the Bible is historical; some characters show forth the glory of God, and some are teachers by bad example. But in all we find our illumination." God teaches through personality, he maintains, citing such Old Testament examples as "Abraham, Joseph, Job, Moses, Joshua,

Samuel, David, Elijah, Jeremiah, Daniel, and the like," together with the apostles and our Lord.

Opposed by such exponents of social religion as Charles Kingsley, this movement nevertheless proved a check to those trends in English Protestantism which have in America continued without challenge. We witness that delayed reaction in American Protestantism now. It is not likely to produce anything comparable to Anglo-Catholicism, but it may be welcomed as a profitable check upon religious anarchism.

More Preparation

While these definite influences are in operation for a wider use of the Christian Year, much more preparation is required before an American Protestant calendar would be universally acceptable. A blind return to the Roman breviary and missal would be neither possible nor desirable. Nor would the Anglican scheme be acceptable in entirely, both containing, as they do, teaching not indigenous to Protestant experience and countless saints either obscure or unknown to Protestants, or whose memories hold no inspiration. On the other hand, these classic patterns, together with the Lutheran, offer a proper base for a beginning and a fruitful field for study.

Should a Protestant commission be created for the purpose of advancing a calendar for general use, its first requirement would be a mastery of the classic trunk lines, upon which basis it would then seek to harmonize and justify the anarchic confusions arising from independent practices of denominations and local churches. Without doubt, every branch of Christendom would have something to add to the ecumenical practices; and in not a few cases traditions of local societies would be found worthy of inclusion in the general program of observances. And, in the last analysis, such an order would remain for Protestantism a voluntary guide rather than an authoritative code. It is hoped that this study may advance the existing trends toward a more unified and historically significant worship.

Particularly, the idea behind the saints' roll offers inviting development for Protestantism. A regular calendar of the great liberal reformers, thinkers, and saints would find a large instructive and devotional use, and would kindle appreciation for the Protestant tradition.

The modern mind can best approach the Church Year by making an objective study of it before attempting its devotional adoption. The latter can come only by slow growth, and perhaps will follow the former by gradual recovery of separate items of the Christian Year—a recovery only so rapid as objective study has made the events significant. This is the process now at work among psychologists in their revived interest in the phenomenon of sainthood. An objective interest in what makes saints behave as they do is, from the religious viewpoint, an advance upon psychology's former scorn of sainthood as simply irrelevant to life. This interest, as expressed in Mecklin's *The Passing of the Saint* and other studies in the psychology or sociology of martyrdom, has promise of redeeming research from its secularity which, in some expressions, has been either indifferent to religion or quite antagonistic. A sympathetic, objective study of saints leads in the direction of devotional fellowship with them.

So the Church Year should be approached by the average Protestant heretofore indifferent to it, or opposed to special celebrations. Beginning with a confession of ignorance, he will find the calendar a fascinating field of discovery which may lead him to put some of the ancient practices to use. Such a revival of an old form is that of the service of Tenebrae—recently brought out from its beginnings in the fourth century A.D.—which has made the Maundy Thursday Communion a richer experience for many Protestants.

Civil Calendar Reform

This rediscovery of the Christian Year has been accompanied by a definite movement for the reform of the current civil calendar, a brief account of which we include here as a note of interest. The Cotsworth calendar is among these newer proposals for replacing the Gregorian, and the Swiss plan is under wide discussion. The beginning of this reform movement may be placed at a convention in Chicago, October 10, 1883. The movement has crystallized into the proposed world calendar, supported by an association organized in many countries and issuing a journal. The time now set for the adoption of this reform is the close of the present war, when it is hoped there will be a world organization which may be utilized in the rapid acceptance of the new plan. The greater need for world-wide unity in time measurement, and the correction of the irregularities of the Gregorian scheme are the main reasons advanced for the change. Advantages offered are: (1) that the same calendar will repeat every year, there being equal quarters and month dates always falling on the same week days; and (2) that it will simplify accounting, regularize holidays, and resolve many confusions in industry, science, and the general social life.

The world calendar divides the year into twelve months, named as at present, each year beginning on Sunday. The first month of each quarter is thirty-one days long, and the other two, thirty days. The year is equalized by a year-end day, December 31, which comes as an extra Saturday each year, and by a leap-year day, June 31, another extra Saturday on leap years. These would be world holidays.

The main bearing of the proposed scheme upon the Christian Year would be in fixing Easter to the same Sunday each year, with the regularization of all the days dependent upon Easter. These and all other celebrations would always fall on the same day of the week in each year. The calendar reform organization has consulted the churches by questionnaire as to any religious issues that might be involved. While there may be sections of Christianity that have come to accept the Nicene tradition of the Easter date as divinely inspired, or now hallowed by custom, a knowledge of the history of the matter would tend to take away the authoritarian character and leave it as a matter of convenience. The change here proposed is not a challenge of an existing culture and offers no violence to ancient usages, but is rather comparable to the device of daylight-saving time in that it seeks a more convenient method. Our purpose is not so much to enter a plea for this reform as to render the sympathetic account which is its due in the general story.

In 1923 the League of Nations Commission on Calendar Reform took action fostering this general program and looking toward the establishment of a fixed Easter. The British Parliament in 1928 passed the so-named "Easter Act," by which, at a time to be designated by orders in Council, Easter would fall on the first Sunday following the second Saturday in April. This should go into effect at a time when uniformity of acceptance by other governments and by the churches could be assured.

Peter Archer, Catholic writer, opposes reform of the Gregorian calendar on the ground that it places commercial utility higher than the religious interests of Jews, Christians, and Mohammedans, and claims that the only reform program that deserves to be called scientific is the thirteen-month calendar.

Experience of the centuries shows that change will not come easily, since, as we have seen, even minor alterations of the calendar are strongly resisted by custom. And, even while these proposals have been advanced, the Gregorian calendar has been extended to China and Russia, finally reaching the status of "world calendar" itself. The coming postwar need for unified time measurement may speed the process which would otherwise consume centuries.

Meantime, the interest in the readjustment of the civil calendar should stimulate the churches toward the better ordering of their religious year.

Chapter XII

VALUES OF AN ORDERED CALENDAR

In this concluding chapter it may be well to re-emphasize the purpose of this book. It is not a proposed authoritative norm for American Protestant worship. The attempt has been to keep it clear of personal whims while at the same time avoiding the appearance of a suggestion that Protestantism restore the full Church Year to use. My concern has been, first of all, to give an account of the history of Christian celebrations, including the present diversification in Protestant usage. Actual practices, rather than proposed innovations, have been the guide. Here I shall indicate some of the values that may be offered by a liberal use of the Christian Year as a *guide* to worship—not an authority over worship.

Dr. Gaius Glenn Atkins in a recent article pointed out that the minister is confronted with three calendars as he plans his preaching and worship: (1) the classic Ecclesiastical Year; (2) the civil calendar, including its American occasions; and (3) the growing accumulation of significant Protestant events. The worship commissions of various denominations and of interchurch councils are concerned with the problem, and they are making progress in bringing Protestant diversities into some sort of unity. This points to no mere restoration of an old order, yet the successful prosecution of the work requires a knowledge of the old together with an appreciation for the new. Meantime the individual minister labors at his task with full use of his traditional Protestant liberty, not unmindful of the discriminating judgment which that freedom demands of him. Intelligent use of an ordered scheme will reveal many values, which I shall here partly summarize.

The Whole Gospel

The whole gospel is emphasized. In the wider rhythm of the Christian Year, the entire first half is given to the revela-

tion of God to man in all its manifestations, the second to human response to the divine initiative. Only in the classic tradition of the historic Church do we find that wholeness of the gospel, simply because all history is required to contain all the parts. Heresy arises when some part is stressed at the expense of the whole, although the particular contention may be true within its limits and in proper setting. For instance, the Pelagian emphasis upon good works certainly showed concern for a great body of Christian truth, the ethical. It became a heresy not in its main emphasis but in its denial of grace. The great tradition contains both grace and ethics, and an exclusive emphasis upon grace would be no more acceptable than the other. Such overspecialized interests are the essence of sectarianism. The Christian Year, as over against these divisive tendencies, has accumulated not only Christian truths but the supplements and complements of each of these truths. Its faithful use is a doctrinal instruction to minister and people and offers redemption from exaggerations, enthusiasms, and inventions. This wholeness of the gospel as conserved in the Christian Year is the main thrust of Howard Chandler Robbins' *Preaching the Gospel.* One would look far for a more effective means of maintaining the full sense of that completeness which is the goal of all human striving and which is found nowhere except in Him who is "perfect and entire, wanting nothing."

Christian Doctrine

The full classic sweep of Christian doctrine is covered in the scope of the Christian Year. Now that Protestantism is

returning to the theological trunk lines, it is important to
remember that theological truth may be conveyed in celebrations as well as in didactics. The preaching of our immediate
past featured the contemporary note, sounded in a vocabulary drawn from secular thought, chiefly psychology and sociology. Under the conditions which bring about neoclassicism this has definitely changed, and the typical Protestant
sermon today deals with the major themes of Christian revelation, somewhat more in the language of theology. The
interest of the modern Church is in what Christianity has to
teach concerning God, man, sin and grace, the Church, the
world, final things. And such themes as these form the staff
upon which is recorded the ceremonial music of the Christian Year.

It is sometimes erroneously said that Trinity Sunday is the
only "doctrinal" day on the calendar. This probably means
it is the only day given directly to the doctrine of the nature
of God. But the wide coverage of theological interests dis-

played in the Christian Year is seen
in the manner in which the clauses
of the Apostles' Creed—the chief symbol of the Church universal—relate
themselves to the various days and
seasons. The Church Year, as Staley
said, "is linked hand in hand with
the Creed. . . . When the Year is neglected the Creed is neglected." Every
article of the Apostles' Creed has its fitting day for special
consideration of its doctrine:

I believe in God the Father Almighty, Maker of heaven and earth
(Trinity Sunday, or the first Sunday in Advent);

and in Jesus Christ his only Son our Lord; who was conceived by the
Holy Ghost, born of the Virgin Mary (Feast of the Nativity, and
the "Mary" days),

suffered under Pontius Pilate, was crucified, dead, and buried (Good
Friday);
the third day he rose again from the dead (Feast of Easter);
he ascended into heaven (Ascension Day),
and sitteth at the right hand of God the Father Almighty (Festival
of Christ the King);
from thence he shall come to judge the quick and the dead (Advent).
I believe in the Holy Ghost (Pentecost),
the holy catholic Church (Whitsuntide),
the communion of saints (All Saints' Day),
the forgiveness of sins (Lent),
the resurrection of the body (All Souls' Day),
And the life everlasting (Easter Day).

The contemporary theologian need not confine his issues to
the exact prescriptions of times and seasons, nor seal his
thinking within the limits of the ancient symbol. But he will
find in the guidance of the liturgical year both support for his
special emphasis and warning against making it exclusive.

Ecumenical Worship

Ecumenical worship is advanced toward a practical unity.
The whole gospel makes for a whole fellowship. True worship may, of course, be had despite great differences. Even
difference in language is no insurmountable barrier. The
delegates to the Oxford Conference, "each in his own
tongue," joined in singing Martin Luther's great hymn, "A
Mighty Fortress Is Our God"; and the very difference of
language added to the depth of meaning in dramatizing the
faith as supranational. But one can hardly say so much for
the inability of Presbyterians and Methodists to engage together in the Lord's Prayer without going to pieces over
"debts" and "trespasses." That sort of disunity has no high
idealism to commend it, and the verbal dissonance is a dis-

tracting, rather than a unifying, experience. Yet, beholden as we are to custom, Congregationalism at Berkeley in 1940 rejected the suggestion of the minister at large, Dr. Horton, to adopt the use of "trespasses" in the interest of the ecu-

menical order, since the majority of Christians use trespasses. If we are not yet ready for so slight a change there is much still to be done before overcoming the larger disjunctions between group practices.

Yet the importance cannot be easily overstressed. We have seen, throughout this brief history of the growth and use of the Church Year, how large a place has been given to the value of unity in worship practices. In most of the controversies concerning dates and usages, the Church universal is heard pleading with a branch of the Church to yield up a group preference in the interest of true catholicity.

The resolution of the many differences in observance will not come by simple majority rule or official decree. In the process each branch of the Church will have something to offer the whole, and even local societies will originate items the universal value of which will be acceptable. This process is going on now, together with the rediscovery of the genius of the Christian Year. As ecumenical worship becomes more a reality there will surely come fitting expression in the more general use of the universal occasions.

Bible Reading

An enormous range of the Bible is covered in the lectionary through which the individual Christian takes his place in the pageantry of the passing Church Year. Not only are Epistles and Gospels indicated for "all the Sundays of

the year," together with the offered texts, but there is a suggested scripture reading for every day of the year. These are selected with a view to covering the whole field of the Bible once in three years. To be sure, a thoroughly studious approach to the Bible would not be confined to the lectionary scheme, but a reading program matching the seasons is superior to the "cover to cover" reading sometimes recommended, and far better than no plan at all. This devotional Bible study, in association with actual events and persons of the Christian Year, has obvious advantages over occasional curious perusal. The devotee who leaves himself to his own devices or to passing inspiration requires an unusual motivation to continue with regularity.

Paradoxically, personal study of the Bible has been neglected in that branch of Christianity whose main original motive was to get back to Scripture, and there is some justification for the comment sometimes made that the Bible is our "least-read best seller." Even in fairly intelligent church circles the ignorance of biblical knowledge is dismaying.

And the subjective, nontextual sermon has offered no encouragement to overcoming the biblical illiteracy in the pew. While the average Protestant would not care to follow the prescript text as an unbreakable rule, he would do well to listen to it at least occasionally as he plans. It may remind him of many homiletic neglects and open new insights.

In the Church Year, minister and people together follow a logical order in a continuing educative and devotional line; and, through the reading they do in common, they come to speak the same language.

The Historic Sense

In the same manner the use of the Church Year cultivates the historic sense. The great richness of its field is a constant invitation to overcome plain ignorance; and its use is a continual discovery of the history of the Church, her great personalities, her struggles, controversies, and conquests.

Every day and season of the year confronts the minister with some aspect of the total life of Christianity which he wants to know more deeply, further study of which yields innumerable homiletic suggestions and enlarges the spiritual life.

The Protestant pulpit presents the paradox of being well informed in secular history but relatively ignorant of church history. Our educated clergy of the present generation have furthered the prophetic accent, which is always the contemporary note with historic overtones. Yet in recent years the historic sense of Protestantism has been nontraditional, or even antitraditional. Its appealing interest has been *social* history rather than *religious* history as such; and its pronouncements, whether of doom or hope, have been extracted from the secular field of studies and uttered in the language of the universities. The criticism that ministers are not informed in secular matters is as ill-founded as it is trite. The average Protestant minister could match libraries with average laymen in any calling; and his conversation is fairly well at home in economics, politics, literature, and the human side of historic movements. It is exactly on the religious side that he needs the undergirding of a wider and wiser information. He has oversimplified his equipment in the history of his own faith. For many Protestants, Christianity begins with the Reformation; and their fund of anecdotes is often exhausted with the stock illustrations of Luther, Wesley, and Calvin, with sometimes a reach back as far as Tyndale, who "defied the pope and all his laws" in giving the English Bible to the plowboys. Yet fifteen fruitful centuries of

193

Christian history precede the Reformation; and it is no yielding of the heritage of the reformers to bring into scope the conquests and controversies, the martyrdoms and mass conversions, of the Church, and her succession of holy men and women that have marched athwart the ages bearing the banners of Christ.

The earliest Christian preaching was steeped in the historic sense. To Peter and Stephen all history was a revelation of the meaning of the covenant between God and man, fulfilled in the crucifixion and resurrection of Christ. And the Church Year, by bringing preachers and lay Christians into the continuing stream of the living tradition, encourages this sense and the power that accompanies it.

Religious Education

The use of the stated calendar is also an aid to effective religious education. Indeed, this is one of the earliest reasons given for the careful definition of the Jewish ceremonies, as Moses remarks after announcing the law concerning observation of the Passover: "And it shall come to pass, when your children shall say unto you, What mean ye by this service?

 that ye shall say, It is the sacrifice of the Lord's Passover, who passed over the houses of the children of Israel in Egypt, when he smote the Egyptians, and delivered our houses." Here is an early recognition of the need for reiteration in the educative process, recently vindicated by a test reported to prove that even university graduate students must be told a thing three times before remembering it. The natural learning method is by way of transmission of a body of experience or social sanctions from the older to the younger generation through the round of repetitive custom. There is no call to surrender the valuable apparatus of mod-

ern educational theory and practice in recognizing the powerful influence of this process on youth. Indeed, we but acknowledge that this takes place prior to, and over and beyond, the conscious and formal educational procedures, and is probably more nearly determinative than the latter.

The observances of the Christian Year recognize this process in periodically confronting the subject with the various elements of religious teaching, thus adding to formal teaching the suggestive power of folk sanctions. Modern religious education, for lack of its appreciation of tradition, broke from the main stream of the Church, with the result that, though encouraging better techniques, it tended to lose religious distinctiveness. The leadership of that movement is now aware of the danger of secularization and is seeking to overcome it by various means. Perhaps one of the chief means at hand is the Christian Year, and religious educators would by its conscious adoption strengthen and deepen the spiritual and social sense of the pupil without sacrificing anything of modern pedagogical gains.

Our American religious leadership, Protestant and Catholic, is just now concerning itself with the problem of unifying secular and religious education. Between the public school system and the church schools the child is subjected to a dual system of values. While there is character education in the public schools, the difference between secular and religious education remains, nonetheless, a large one. That something should be done to offer the child a unifying experience is now recognized by the best leadership in both systems, although the means for accomplishing this are still under debate. The "released time" program of weekday religious education—as developed at Gary, Indiana, some years ago and recently extended to St. Louis, New York, and Chicago—is one answer.

It is of special interest in this study that another preferred approach by some of the most advanced of the religious educators points toward a partial revival of the Christian Year as the best means of meeting the problem. The proposal is that church school and public school join together in public celebrations. This would be undertaken not by an uncritical return to discarded solemnities but under conscious controls and with selection of the values of the common culture which are thought worthy of conserving and extending. In this effort the intellectualist suspicion of formalism must be set aside. Ceremonial practices do not guarantee desirable public religion, but certainly a religious culture cannot long survive the abandonment of the practices of religious culture. If the aim of our education is the cultivation of religious and democratic attitudes and the unification of the child in the common culture, there are few better means at hand than the ceremonial, "for children and ordinary folk understand the meaning of solemnities."

Long-Range Planning

The value of long-range planning is encouraged by intelligent use of the Christian Year. The libertarian suspicion against set schemes as enslaving falls in turn under the criticism of anarchism, as in every field of modern life ordered planning is the mode. This has very special reference to the preacher's task, and the day is already far gone in which the sermon program was supposed to fall together haphazardly out of the preacher's chance inspirations. In recognition of the processional dignity of religion, we now "see our year as a whole." True, a man may be the slave of any blueprint, but he may also be its master. And servitude to planlessness is hardly better than uncritical acceptance of a mechanical program. The proper use of routine is precisely in setting one free. He who carefully plans his arrangements in advance and, through well-ordered habit, reduces to routine the things that belong to routine, is the more at liberty to meet the unforeseen contemporary event which is the subject matter of all prophetic preaching. The plan, of course, must be flexible enough to allow for that. And one of the merits of the

Christian Year is its allowance of variety while making for constancy. Indeed, the calendar items for any given Sunday

and its near days present the problem of culling out what will not be used.

By use of the Church Year the minister anticipates the seasons and may arrange his sermons in effective series, developing whole fields of Christian thought rather than throwing out unrelated ideas week by week. This series planning is recommended as better for the congregation as well as for the minister. Besides saving the preacher the wear and tear on his originality, it brings the man and congregation together in a continuing seasonal experience, follows an educative line to logical outcomes, and unifies the common devotion.

The fear that the guidance of the Christian Year might make for an endless round of consecutive texts, boring to congregation and paralyzing to the preacher, is ill founded. The suggested themes are broad enough to allow for an almost infinite variety of treatment. The same season may, in successive years, become the occasion for a series of expository sermons upon one of the Gospels, or a series on well-chosen heroes of the faith, or on some aspect of Christian doctrine. Year after year, the imaginative preacher would return to the same great occasions with fresh insights and original treatment.

And perhaps the lack of a sense of need for the guidance of a general plan is a manifestation of self-sufficiency not always justified in the performance. Exceptional spiritual geniuses may find their own inner resources sufficient for the regular production of preaching of a high level. But there is still the need of the masses for instructive reiteration under direction. An ideal norm is thus offered the honest minister who would look ahead to his planning, or back upon his themes and emphases to find what he has omitted and what played upon out of proportion. Submitting one's private inspirations to the norm of the Ecclesiastical Year may prove an enriching humility.

Personal and Social Needs

Finally, personal and social needs and duties of Christians are met by use of the Christian Year. The gospel is simple, but its ramifications are complex. And the wide variety of personal religious needs will almost surely be neglected where they are not served through the repetitive order. The whole of a man's ministry may fall into the realm of moral challenge, for instance, while he almost totally neglects the need of many of his hearers for comfort in sickness and death, for courage and strength in weakness, or for intimate instruction in prayer or in the Bible. What was said in relation to the whole gospel is applicable here. The preacher who stresses the social aspects of religion to the neglect of the personal, or the personal at the expense of the social, or otherwise plays his homiletic piece upon one string, violates the patience of his folk as well as disregards their vast variety of spiritual needs.

The great social concerns recur throughout the Christian Year and have their special season at Kingdomtide. There, twelve weeks straight may properly be devoted to the contemporary emphasis upon ethical problems, or to studies in the social implications in the Gospels and Letters. As we have seen, great special occasions at intervals bring particular concerns to the fore, reinforcing the sermon with the celebration. Prophetic vision and passion stir throughout the seasons if their conduct is in the hands of a prophet. He who follows the Church Year has no call to neglect the immense ethical concerns of labor, race, brotherhood, interfaith, and so forth.

But the separate person is not forgotten, but rather

dignified in being given a part to play in the redemptive drama. He is given the benefit of guidance in his meditative life and aided by tradition in the devotions between Sundays. Personal devotion runs very thin when, suspicious of all formalities, persons deprive their quiet hours of external means and helps. One can hardly avoid the errors of subjectivity and superficiality when praying alone and uninstructed. And he can hardly fall into them when his daily prayer brings him faithfully and habitually into the guidance of the ages. The separate Christian deserves more help than Protestantism has usually given him, and he should not be thrown upon his own resources without the means at hand for reinforcing his own with the resources of the wider Christian experience.

In recognition of this need, the great events of human life are given sacramental value and a place in the general scheme, appropriate times being offered for celebrations or commemorations of birth, baptism, confirmation, marriage, death, either through days appointed for the proper rites or through their inclusion in the emphasis of the various home and family days.

We should allay the intellectualist fear that by this means superstition would be cultivated in the ignorant. The ignorant are not the only ones! There are superstitions which belong peculiarly to the sophisticated, and one of them is a blind belief in the validity of one's own opinions and conclusions. It is true that religion and superstition are strangely interblended. Yet if our concern for the ignorant is genuine, we will recognize that their enlightenment comes more through social acceptances than through philosophical formulations or pedagogical processes—which are themselves symbolic. And the modern intelligence should be open to the question whether the humble and sincere devotion of simple souls takes precedence over the intellectual pride of those who, ridding themselves of superstition, have damaged their belief in all things.

The superstitious regard for saints' days is illustrated by

the following tale told by Prince Alexis Obolensky, former
procurator of the holy synod in Russia, to the "Gentleman
with a duster" and recounted by him in *Painted Windows*:

A man set out one winter's night to murder an old woman in her
cottage. As he tramped through the snow with the hatchet under his
blouse, it suddenly occurred to him that it was a *Saints' Day*.
Instantly he dropped on his knees in the snow, crossed himself
violently with trembling hands, and in a guilty voice implored God
to forgive him for his evil intention, *postponing the murder until
the next night*.

An amusing anecdote, and not without point. But, besides
revealing the superstition which may accompany all religious
observances, it really shows that commemorations are in some
measure deterrents to wrongdoing. And, further, the story
neglects to point out that every day is some saints' day,
which, had the man known it, would have spoiled tomorrow
and all succeeding days as appropriate for crime. Certainly,
had he no upbringing at all in the practices of devotion, his
moral situation would not necessarily have been improved.

The Christian Year meets the individual upon whatever
level he occupies in the infinite scales or in moral and spiritual
capacity.

The Year as a Whole

Here a modern littérateur expresses his appreciation. It
is Franz Werfel in *Embezzled Heaven*, a story cast in the
setting of the ecclesiastical devotions as celebrated at St.
Peter's in Rome. For the author, as well as for the humble
serving woman whose life he portrays, the symbols and ceremonies of the ancient Christian Year convey the eternal
meanings according to capacity to receive them. He writes:

The cycle of the ecclesiastical year mirrors on a divine plane the
cycle of the earthly year. Just as the latter contains its seasons of
blossoming trees, cutting of the corn, gathering of the vine, and

fall of the snow, so does the former its succession of feast-days in constant recapitulation. And as the man who lives close to nature shares with his body and soul in the seasonal course of the earthly year, the pious believer participates in the eternally unchanging round of the ecclesiastical year. They bloom and ripen and fade in accordance with the varying phases of the earthly and divine suns.[1]

The comparison is suggestive. The floodlights of heaven play upon the sober pageantry of human destiny. The wheel of history's universe turns about its Center. Multitudes of men and choirs of angels glorify the Author of Events, and all things in time and space are baptized in meaning by the Light of the World. Every ground is holy, and each year *anno Domini*, the "year of our Lord," its beginning inscribed, as Bach's immortal scores, "To the glory of God," and signed as the great composer signed his every composition, "In the name of Christ. Amen."

[1] New York: The Viking Press, 1940. Used by permission.

201

ALL THE SUNDAYS IN THE YEAR

CALENDAR OF FIXED DAYS

SELECTED BIBLIOGRAPHY

INDEX

SPECIAL ABBREVIATIONS

A   All denominations
E   Protestant Episcopal
Ep.   Epistle (or a substitute therefor)
Go.   Gospel
L   Lutheran
P   Protestant
R   Roman Catholic

ALL THE SUNDAYS IN THE YEAR

FIRST HALF OF THE CHURCH YEAR

Advent through Pentecost
(Sunday nearest Nov. 30 through seventh Sunday after Easter)

God Speaking to Man Through Revelation

---◄{ ADVENT }►---

Advent Sunday through Christmas Eve

Expectancy of the Coming of Christ

PURPLE

ADVENT SUNDAY (purple), or First Sunday in Advent—Sunday nearest
St. Andrew's Day (Nov. 30)
Ep. Rom. 13:8-14 *(A)* Preparation for Coming Light
Go. Matt. 21:1-9 *(E, L)* Triumphal Entry
Luke 21:25-33 *(R)* Signs in the Sun

SECOND SUNDAY IN ADVENT (purple): Universal Bible Sunday
Ep. Rom. 15:4-12 *(A)* Prophecy Fulfilled
Go. Matt. 11:2-10 *(R)* John Baptist's Question
Luke 21:25-33 *(E, L)* Signs in the Sun

THIRD SUNDAY IN ADVENT (purple or rose): Mid-Advent; Gaudete
Sunday
Ep. I Cor. 4:1-5 *(E, L)* Of Ministers and Stewards
Phil. 4:4-7 *(R)* Rejoice in the Lord
Go. Matt. 11:2-10 *(E, L)* John Baptist's Question
John 1:19-28 *(R)* The Baptist's Preparation

FOURTH SUNDAY IN ADVENT (purple): Sunday Before Christmas; Rorate
Sunday
Ep. I Cor. 4:1-5 *(R)* Of Ministers and Stewards
Phil. 4:4-7 *(E, L)* Rejoice in the Lord

205

Go. Luke 3:1-6 *(R)* The Preaching of John
John 1:19-28 *(E, L)* The Baptist's Preparation

─────────── ⚜{ CHRISTMASTIDE }⚜ ───────────

Christmas Day through Epiphany Eve
(Dec. 25 through Jan. 5)

The Nativity, the Incarnation, and the Christian Prospect

WHITE

CHRISTMAS DAY (white), or Nativity of Our Lord, or Birthday of
Christ—Incarnation
  Ep. Isa. 9:2-7 *(L)* Light in Darkness
    Titus 2:11-15 *(A)* The Grace of God
    Heb. 1:12 *(A)* Heir of All Things
  Go. Luke 2:1-14 *(A)* The Birth of Jesus
    Luke 2:15-20 *(L, R)* The Shepherd Story.
    John 1:1-14 *(A)* In the Beginning the Word

FIRST SUNDAY AFTER CHRISTMAS DAY (white), or Sunday Within the
Octave of Christmas
  Ep. Gal. 4:1-7 *(A)* The Adoption of Sons
  Go. Matt. 1:18-25 *(E)* The Birth of Jesus
    Luke 2:33-40 *(L, R)* The Blessing of Simeon

CIRCUMCISION OF CHRIST (white), or Circumcision and Name of Jesus:
Octavus Domini (as falling upon the octave of Christmas); New
Year's Day
  Ep. Gal. 3:23-29 *(L)* Faith and the Law
    Phil. 2:9-13 *(E)* The Name
    Titus 2:11-15 *(R)* The Grace of God
  Go. Luke 2:15-20 *(E)* The Shepherd Story
    Luke 2:21 *(L, R)* The Name

SECOND SUNDAY AFTER CHRISTMAS DAY (white), or Sunday Between
the Circumcision and the Epiphany, or *(R)* Feast of the Most Holy
Name of Jesus
  Ep. Isa. 61:1-3 *(E)* Good Tidings to the Poor
    Acts 4:8-12 *(R)* No Other Name
    I Pet. 4:12-19 *(L)* Fiery Trials
  Go. Matt. 2:13-23 *(E, L)* Joseph's Dream in Egypt
    Luke 2:21 *(R)* The Name

ALL THE SUNDAYS IN THE YEAR

⸻⸻⸺⸽ EPIPHANY SEASON ⸾⸺⸻⸻

THEOPHANY SEASON

Epiphany through Septuagesima Sunday Eve

(Jan. 6 through eve of third Sunday before Lent)

The tendency in the evangelical churches is to include the short pre-Lenten season in the Season of Epiphany, in which case the present season extends to Ash Wednesday.

Manifestations of Our Lord; Christian Missions

GREEN

EPIPHANY, or Manifestation of Christ to the Gentiles (white): Old Christmas; Twelfth Day; Feast of the Three Kings; Feast of the Baptism of Christ; Theophany (Eastern Church)
Ep. Isa. 60:1-6 *(L, R)* Thy Light Is Come
  Eph. 3:1-12 *(E)* Fellow Heirs
Go. Matt. 2:1-12 *(A)* The Coming of the Wise Men

FIRST SUNDAY AFTER EPIPHANY (white), or Sunday Within the Octave of Epiphany; Feast of the Holy Family *(R)*; Missions Sunday *(P)*
Ep. Rom. 12:1-5 *(L, E)* A Living Sacrifice
  Col. 3:12-17 *(R)* Christian Virtues
Go. Luke 2:41-52 *(A)* Christ in the Temple

SECOND SUNDAY AFTER EPIPHANY (green): Missionary Day
Ep. Rom. 12:6-16 *(A)* Diversity of Gifts
Go. Mark 1:1-11 *(E)* Preparation of John Baptist
  John 2:1-11 *(L, R)* The Marriage Supper

THIRD SUNDAY AFTER EPIPHANY (green)
Ep. Rom. 12:16-21 *(A)* Overcoming Evil with Good
Go. Matt. 8:1-13 *(L, R)* Cleansing of the Leper
  John 2: 1-11 *(P, E)* The Marriage Supper

FOURTH SUNDAY AFTER EPIPHANY (green)
Ep. Rom. 13:1-10 *(A)* The Powers That Be
Go. Matt. 8:1-13 *(E)* Cleansing of the Leper
  Matt. 8:23-27 *(L, R)* Stilling the Storm

FIFTH SUNDAY AFTER EPIPHANY (green)
Ep. Col. 3:12-17 *(A)* Christian Virtues
Go. Matt. 13:24-30 *(A)* Tares and Wheat

SIXTH SUNDAY AFTER EPIPHANY (green)

The Lutheran Service Book omits this service, celebrating instead the Transfiguration of Our Lord. The Catholic and Episcopal Transfiguration is on August 6.

Ep. I Thess. 1:2-10 *(R)* Fruit of the Gospel
I John 3:1-8 *(E)* Sons of God
Go. Matt. 13:24-30 *(R)* Mustard Seed
Matt. 24:23-31 *(E)* False Christs

TRANSFIGURATION OF OUR LORD (used by the Lutherans as the last Sunday after Epiphany)

Ep. II Pet. 1:16-21 *(L)* Eyewitnesses of His Majesty
Go. Matt. 17:1-9 *(L)* The Transfiguration

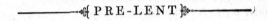

PRE-LENT

SEPTUAGESIMA SEASON

The three Sundays before Ash Wednesday
(Protestants frequently include this season in the Epiphany Season.)

The Battle of the Spirit

PURPLE OR GREEN

The color is purple when Lenten emphasis is used; it is green when the season is considered as continuing Epiphany.

SUNDAY CALLED SEPTUAGESIMA (purple or green), or Septuagesima Sunday, or Third Sunday Before Lent—also Lost Sunday because of its transitional position between Epiphany Season and Lent and because for a long time it was without a name
Ep. I Cor. 9:24–10:5 *(A)* Running the Race
Go. Matt. 20:1-16 *(A)* Laborers in the Vineyard

SUNDAY CALLED SEXAGESIMA (purple or green), or Sexagesima Sunday, or Second Sunday before Lent (Apokreos Sunday in the Greek Church)
Ep. II Cor. 11:19–12:9 *(A)* Perils of Paul
Go. Luke 8:4-15 *(A)* Parable of the Sower

SUNDAY CALLED QUINQUAGESIMA (purple or green), or Quinquagesima Sunday, or Sunday Next Before Lent
Ep. I Cor. 13:1-13 *(A)* Hymn to Love
Go. Luke 18:31-43 *(A)* The Way to Jerusalem

SHROVE MONDAY, or Collop Monday—Monday before Ash Wednesday

This was the early feast day before the final fast of Lent, of more social than religious significance, and now obsolete. The "collops" were the choice meat morsels which made a part of the regular menu.

SHROVE TUESDAY, or Shrovetide—Tuesday before Ash Wednesday

Originally the day of penitence, or "shriving," it later became a time of merrymaking and feasting. It is called Carnival Day in Italy, the word coming from the Latin meaning "farewell to meat." In France, and in New Orleans, it is the famous Mardi Gras, or Fat Tuesday, of general popular celebration.

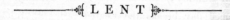

-------------✦{ L E N T }✦--------------

LENTENTIDE, or QUADRAGESIMA SEASON

Ash Wednesday through Easter Eve
(The forty days, not including Sundays, before Easter)
Self Examination, Penitence, and Renewal

PURPLE

ASH WEDNESDAY (purple), or First Day of Lent—forty days before Easter, not including Sundays
Ep. Joel 2:12-19 *(A)* Rend Your Hearts
Go. Matt. 6:16-21 *(A)* When Ye Fast

WORLD DAY OF PRAYER—first Friday of Lent

This day is a contribution to the Christian Year by Protestant women. It is sponsored by the National Committee of Church Women, representing various missionary bodies. Large gatherings are held, in the Lenten spirit, with central emphasis on the world-wide concern of Christians.

FIRST SUNDAY IN LENT (purple): Shrove Sunday; Invocavit Sunday— beginning of Clean Lent, as distinct from pre-Lent
Ep. II Cor. 6:1-10 *(A)* The Discipline of Grace
Go. Matt. 4:1-11 *(A)* Temptation in the Wilderness

SPRING EMBER DAYS *(E, R)*—Wednesday, the octave of Ash Wednesday, together with the Friday and Saturday following

Derived from *quator tempora*—"four times"—and marked off to celebrate each incoming season of the natural year, they are proper times for ordination to the ministry or other church office.

Ep. Acts 13:44-49 *(E)* The Word of God
Go. Luke 4:16-21 *(E)* Jesus Preaches in the Synagogue

SECOND SUNDAY IN LENT (purple): Reminiscere Sunday
Ep. I Thess. 4:1-7 *(A)* Call to Holiness

Go. Matt. 15:21-28 *(E, L)* Canaanite Woman's Daughter
Matt. 17:1-9 *(R)* The Transfiguration

THIRD SUNDAY IN LENT (purple): Oculi Sunday
Ep. Eph. 5:1-9 *(A)* Followers of God
Go. Luke 11:14-28 *(A)* Casting Out the Dumb Devil

FOURTH SUNDAY IN LENT (purple or rose): Mid-Lent; Laetare Sunday; Mothering Sunday; Refreshment Sunday; Simnel Sunday; Rose Sunday; Jerusalem Sunday; New Sunday; Alb Sunday

This much-named day breaks the Lenten fast with rejoicing. It was, in England, a home-coming day, a forerunner of Mothers' Day, and a time of refreshment and feasting on "simnel" cakes. The prayer of the day is one of gratitude for forgiveness, and grateful recognition is given of the grace that brings relief from punishment, however much deserved. Parts of Protestantism use the day as Stewardship Sunday.

Ep. Gal. 4:21-31 *(A)* Justification by Faith
Go. John 6:1-15 *(A)* Feeding the Five Thousand

PASSIONTIDE
The last two weeks in Lent

PASSION WEEK
Passion Sunday through Palm Sunday Eve

PASSION SUNDAY (purple), or Fifth Sunday in Lent; Judica Sunday; Care Sunday; Black Sunday
Ep. Heb. 9:11-15 *(A)* Redemptive Suffering
Go. John 8:46-59 *(A)* Jesus' Colloquy with Accusers

FRIDAY IN PASSION WEEK (white—*R* only) Feast of the Seven Dolors of the B.V.M. (remembering the seven great griefs in the life of Mary)

HOLY WEEK
GREAT WEEK
Palm Sunday through Easter Eve

PALM SUNDAY (purple), or Sunday Before Easter; Palmarum; Sixth Sunday in Lent; Sallow Sunday; Sunday of Branches; Tradition Sunday (because the Apostles' Creed was thought to have been given on or about Palm Sunday)

Ep. Exod. 15:27–16:7 *(R)* Manna in the Wilderness
Phil. 2:5-11 *(A)* The Mind Which Was in Christ
Go. Matt. 21:1-9 *(L, R)* The Triumphal Entry
Matt. 26:1-75–27:1-66 *(L)* The Passion
Matt. 27:1-54 *(E)* The Passion

MONDAY BEFORE EASTER (purple), or Monday in Holy Week
Ep. Isa. 5:5-10 *(R)* God, My Helper
Isa. 50:5-10 *(L)* Trust in God
Isa. 63:1-19 *(E)* Judgment and Grace
Go. Mark 14:1-30 *(E)* The Passion
John 12:1-23 *(L, R)* The Triumphal Entry, or The History of
the Passion

TUESDAY BEFORE EASTER (purple), or Tuesday in Holy Week
Ep. Jer. 11:18-28 *(L, R)* Lamb to the Slaughter
Isa. 50:5-10 *(E)* Trust in God
Go. Mark 14:15-46 *(R)* The Passion
Mark 15:1-39 *(E)* The Passion
John 12:24-43 *(L)* A Grain of Wheat, or The History of the
Passion

WEDNESDAY BEFORE EASTER (purple), or Wednesday in Holy Week; Spy
Wednesday (as on this day Judas made arrangement for the betrayal)
Ep. Isa. 53:1-12 *(R)* Man of Sorrows
Isa. 62:11–63:7 *(L, R)* The Saviour Cometh
Heb. 9:16-28 *(E)* The Sacrifice
Go. Luke 22:1-71 *(E, L)* The Passion
Luke 22:1–23:53 *(R)* The Passion

MAUNDY THURSDAY (purple, if communion is not celebrated; white, with
communion), or Thursday before Easter, or Thursday in Holy Week;
Shore Thursday (from the shorn heads of the priests); sometimes
Holy Thursday (although this is also applied to Corpus Christi Day,
and more commonly to Ascension Day)

Ep. I Cor. 11:23-32 *(A)* The Holy Communion
Go. Luke 23:1-49 *(E)* The Passion
John 13:1-15 *(A)* The New Commandment, or The History of
the Passion *(L)*

The Vigil of Maundy Thursday, or the Office of Tenebrae with Holy Communion, is a Protestant adaptation of a service dating from the fourth century. In Catholic use it is observed on Wednesday, Thursday, and Friday of
Holy Week at Matins and Lauds. It is finding wide use among the evangelical
churches for the pre-Easter Communion.

GOOD FRIDAY (black)
Ep. Exod. 12:1-11 *(R)* The Passover
    Isa. 52:13–53:12 *(L)* Prophecy of Christ's Glory
    Heb. 10:1-25 *(E)* The Sufficient Sacrifice
Go. John 18:1–19:42 *(L, R)* The Passion
    John 19:1-37 *(P)* The Passion, or The History of the Passion *(L)*

Passion Hours, is one Protestant service following the mode of devotional gatherings by communities, during the three hours—from noon until three—that Jesus hung on the cross. Such services have grown greatly in use, and are now observed in almost every community. The Seven Last Words are used.

SATURDAY IN HOLY WEEK (no color): Holy Saturday; The Great Sabbath; Easter Even; The Vigil of Easter Day

Precisely speaking, Easter Even is the interlude between the close of Lent, at noon, and the dawn of Easter Day.

Ep. I Pet. 3:17-22 *(E)* The Benefits of Christ
Go. Matt. 27:57-66 *(E)* When Even Was Come

───────────────◆{ EASTERTIDE }◆───────────────

Easter Day to Ascension Day

A forty-day season corresponding to the forty days of Lent, the biblical time between the Resurrection and the Ascension. The Feast of Easter is kept in the Roman Church to Pentecost.

The Risen Lord
WHITE

In the transition between these seasons it is important to note the position of Easter as the *beginning* of *Eastertide,* rather than the *close* of *Lent.* The theme of the Resurrection pervades the joyful atmosphere of these coming weeks. When congregations are instructed in this meaning it will mean much in overcoming the treatment of the season as an anticlimactic post-Easter.

EASTER DAY (white), or Easter Sunday; Resurrection of Our Lord; God's Sunday; Great Sunday; Holy Sunday—in the Greek Church begins New Week.

Falls on the Sunday after the first full moon on or after March 21: the earliest possible date, March 22; the latest, April 25.

Ep. I Cor. 5:6-8 *(A)* The Old Leaven Purged
    Col. 3:1-3 *(E)* Risen With Christ
Go. Mark 16:1-8 *(A)* He Is Risen
    John 20:1-10 *(E)* The First Day of the Week

MONDAY IN EASTER WEEK, or Easter Monday; Monday after Easter.
Ep. Acts 10:34-41 *(E, L)* Peter's Testimony
Go. Luke 24:13-35 *(E, L)* The Road to Emmaus

TUESDAY IN EASTER WEEK, or Easter Tuesday *(E* only)
Ep. Acts 13:26-41 *(E)* Paul at Antioch
Go. Luke 24:36-48 *(E)* Jesus' Appearance

FIRST SUNDAY AFTER EASTER (white): Quasi Modo Geniti Sunday; Low Sunday (by contrast with the "high" Easter Day—the beginning of Low Week); White Sunday (because white is the seasonal color, although this term properly belongs to Whitsunday)

> Another folk usage is Second First Sunday, the *first* First Sunday being the First Sunday after the Epiphany.

Ep. I John 5:4-12 *(A)* The Victory That Overcometh
Go. John 20:19-31 *(A)* Jesus in the Midst

SECOND SUNDAY AFTER EASTER (white): Misericordias Domini Sunday; Shepherd Sunday; Renewal Sunday
Ep. I Pet. 2:19-25 *(A)* Like Sheep Astray
Go. John 10:11-16 *(A)* The Good Shepherd

> Lord's Day Alliance Day—the second Sunday after Easter—is promoted by the Lord's Day Alliance to emphasize the sanctity of Sunday.
> Youth Sunday—some Sunday in Eastertide. This is a recent addition to the Church Year as practiced in Protestantism. It is greatly in need of regularization, since the dates and types of observation vary widely.
> Vocation Sunday—some Sunday in Eastertide. This, too, is a recent addition, not yet widely observed but growing in interest. It seeks to stress the Christian teaching concerning life-work.

THIRD SUNDAY AFTER EASTER (white): Jubilate Sunday (in the Eastern Church, Myrrhophori Sunday)
Ep. I Pet. 2:11-20 *(A)* Christian Discipline
Go. John 16:16-23 *(A)* A Little While

FOURTH SUNDAY AFTER EASTER (white): Cantate Sunday. (May be appropriately observed as a festival of sacred music and hymns)
Ep. Jas. 1:16-21 *(A)* Every Good and Perfect Gift
Go. John 16:5-15 *(A)* I Go to My Father

ROGATION SUNDAY (green, if "rural life" theme is used; purple, otherwise), or Fifth Sunday after Easter; Rogate Sunday

> This Sunday before the Rogation Days, is given to the subject of prayer, and the spirit combines great joy and solemnity. It is the traditional Sunday

for "perambulation of the parish," or "beating the bounds," while the faithful, accompanying the pastor, walk the whole circuit of the charge.

In Protestant usage the Fifth Sunday is widely used as Rural Life Sunday.

Ep. Jas. 1:22-27 *(A)* Doers of the Word

Go. John 16:23-30 *(A)* Whatsoever Ye Ask

ROGATION DAYS (purple), or Gang Days (Monday, Tuesday, and Wednesday immediately preceding Ascension Day)

These days were established in a time of earthquake and terror in A.D. 460-470 under Bishop Mamertus. Catholics offer Mass on each of the days.

⊶⊰ ASCENSIONTIDE ⊱⊷

Ascension Day through the Sunday within the octave of the Ascension

The Ascended Lord

WHITE

ASCENSION DAY (white): Ascension of Our Lord; Holy Thursday—forty days after Easter

Ep. Acts 1:1-11 *(A)* The Ascension.

Go. Mark 16:14-20 *(L, R)* The Ascension

Luke 24:49-53 *(E)* The Ascension

SUNDAY AFTER ASCENSION DAY (white), or Sunday Within the Octave of the Ascension; Exaudi Sunday; Expectation Sunday

Ep. I Pet. 4:7-11 *(A)* The End of All Things

Go. John 15:26—16:4a *(A)* The Comforter Is Come

⊶⊰ WHITSUNTIDE ⊱⊷

WHITSUNWEEK

Whitsunday or Pentecost to the End of the Week

The Emerging Church

RED

Catholic practice begins the second half of the year with Pentecost, the Lutherans and Episcopalians with Trinity Sunday. Both designations will be shown, as, for instance, the Twelfth Sunday after Pentecost being also designated as the Eleventh Sunday after Trinity.

Bearing in mind the major themes of the year halves; first, "God speaking to man through revelation," and second, "Man responding to God through commitment," Pentecost properly belongs to both. It is God's last word to man in the gift of the Spirit; it is also man's answer to God in the ongoing life of the Church.

WHITSUNDAY (red), or Pentecost: Festival of Pentecost; Birthday of the Church; White Sunday; Pascha Rosatum, or Feast of Roses

This is one of the oldest of the Christian celebrations, going back to the three principal feasts of Judaism. It is elaborately celebrated in the older churches, and its use is being strongly revived in Protestantism as a time of emphasizing the Church.

Ep. Acts 2:1-13 *(A)* The Day of Pentecost
I Cor. 12:4-14 *(E)* Diversity of Gifts
Go. Luke 11:9-13 *(E)* Ask, Seek, Knock
John 14:15-31 *(A)* Keep My Commandments

MONDAY IN WHITSUNWEEK
Ep. Acts 10:34-48 *(E, L)* Peter's Preaching
Go. John 3:16-21 *(E, L)* God's Supreme Gift

TUESDAY IN WHITSUNWEEK
Ep. Acts 8:14-17 *(E)* The Holy Ghost
Go. John 10:1-10 *(E)* Parable of the Sheepfold

SUMMER EMBER DAYS: Wednesday, Friday, and Saturday after Pentecost

SECOND HALF OF THE CHURCH YEAR

Trinity Sunday through the Sunday next before Advent

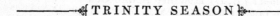

───────◄{TRINITY SEASON}►───────

Entire second half of the Church Year

Man responding to God through commitment

GREEN (E, L) OR WHITE (R)

TRINITY SUNDAY (white): Festival of the Holy Trinity; First Sunday after Pentecost; or Sunday Next After Pentecost
Ep. Rom. 11:33-36 *(L, R)* The Depth of the Riches
I John 4:8-21 *(R)* God Is Love
Rev. 4:1-11 *(E)* A Throne Set in Heaven

Go. Luke 6:36-42 *(R)* Be Ye Merciful
John 3:1-15 *(E, L)* Ye Must Be Born Again

FEAST OF CORPUS CHRISTI (white) *(R)* Thursday after Trinity Sunday—
sometimes on First Sunday after Trinity
Ep. I Cor. 11:23-29 *(R)* Institution of the Holy Communion
Go. John 6:56-59 *(R)* Bread of Heaven

FIRST SUNDAY AFTER TRINITY *(E, L;* green), or Second Sunday After
Pentecost *(R;* white); Sunday Within the Octave of Corpus Christi
(R; white)
Ep. I John 3:13-18 *(R)* Love, the Test
I John 4:7-21 *(E, L)* The Spirit and Love
Go. Luke 14:15-24 *(R)* Parable of the Supper
Luke 16:19-31 *(E, L)* Parable of Lazarus and the Rich Man

FRIDAY AFTER THE OCTAVE OF CORPUS CHRISTI *(R;* white): Feast of the
Sacred Heart of Jesus

SECOND SUNDAY AFTER TRINITY *(E, L;* green), or Third Sunday After
Pentecost *(R;* white)
Ep. I Pet. 5:5-11 *(R)* Humility Before God
I John 3:13-18 *(E, L)* Love, the Test
Go. Luke 14:16-24 *(E, L)* Parable of the Supper
Luke 15:1-14 *(R)* The Lost Sheep and the Lost Coin

THIRD SUNDAY AFTER TRINITY *(E, L;* green), or Fourth Sunday After
Pentecost *(R;* white)
Ep. Rom. 8:18-23 *(R)* Present Sufferings, Future Glory
I Pet. 5:5-11 *(E, L)* Humility Before God
Go. Luke 5:1-11 *(R)* Fishers of Men
Luke 15:1-10 *(E, L)* Lost Sheep

FOURTH SUNDAY AFTER TRINITY *(E, L;* green), or Fifth Sunday After
Pentecost *(R;* white)
Ep. Rom. 8:18-23 *(E, L)* Present Sufferings, Future Glory
I Pet. 3:8-15 *(R)* All of One Mind
Go. Matt. 5:20-24 *(R)* Except Your Righteousness Exceed
Luke 6:36-42 *(E, L)* Be Ye Merciful

FIFTH SUNDAY AFTER TRINITY *(E, L;* green), or Sixth Sunday After
Pentecost *(R;* white)

Ep. Rom. 6:3-11 *(R)* Buried with Christ
I Pet. 3:8-15 *(E, L)* All of One Mind
Go. Mark 8:1-9 *(R)* Feeding the Multitude
Luke 5:1-11 *(E, L)* Fishers of Men

SIXTH SUNDAY AFTER TRINITY *(E, L;* green), or Seventh Sunday After
Pentecost *(R;* white)
Ep. Rom. 6:3-11 *(E, L)* Buried with Christ
Rom. 6:19-23 *(R)* A Human Thing
Go. Matt. 5:20-26 *(E, L)* Except Your Righteousness Exceed
Matt. 7:15-21 *(R)* False Prophets

SEVENTH SUNDAY AFTER TRINITY *(E, L;* green), or Eighth Sunday After
Pentecost *(R;* white)
Ep. Rom. 6:19-23 *(E, L)* A Human Thing
Rom. 8:12-17 *(R)* We Are Debtors
Go. Mark 8:1-9 *(E, L)* Feeding the Multitude
Luke 16:1-9 *(R)* Parable of the Steward

EIGHTH SUNDAY AFTER TRINITY *(E, L;* green), or Ninth Sunday After
Pentecost *(R;* white)
Ep. Rom. 8:12-17 *(E, L)* We Are Debtors
I Cor. 10:6-13 *(R)* Bearing Temptation
Go. Matt. 7:15-23 *(E, L)* False Prophets
Luke 19:41-47 *(R)* Jesus Weeps over Jerusalem

NINTH SUNDAY AFTER TRINITY *(E, L;* green), or Tenth Sunday After
Pentecost *(R;* white)
Ep. I Cor. 10:1-13 *(E, L)* Bearing Temptation
I Cor. 12:2-11 *(R)* Manifestations of the Spirit
Go. Luke 15:11-32 *(E)* The Prodigal Son
Luke 16:1-9 *(L)* Parable of the Steward
Luke 18:9-14 *(R)* Parable of the Pharisee and the Publican

KINGDOMTIDE

Last Sunday in August through the Sunday Next Before Advent

This subseason within the Season of Trinity is a recent Protestant introduction, promoted by the Federal Council of Churches. The Catholic Festival of
Christ the King falls on the last Sunday in October, which in Protestant usage
is Reformation Sunday. The custom here noted is for information rather than
direction, it being still a matter of discussion as to its liturgical fitness at
this time.

217

FESTIVAL OF CHRIST THE KING *(P;* white)
Ep. *Col.* 1:12-20 *(P)* The Kingdom of the Son
Go. John 18:33-37 *(P)* Thou Sayest that I Am a King

TENTH SUNDAY AFTER TRINITY *(E, L;* green), or Eleventh Sunday After
Pentecost *(R;* white)
Ep. I Cor. 12:1-11 *(E, L)* Manifestations of the Spirit
I Cor. 15:1-10 *(R)* The Gospel of Christ
Go. Mark 7:31-37 *(R)* Healing of One Deaf and Dumb
Luke 19:41-48 *(E, L)* Jesus Weeps over Jerusalem

ELEVENTH SUNDAY AFTER TRINITY *(E, L;* green), or Twelfth Sunday
After Pentecost *(R)* white)
Ep. I Cor. 15:1-10 *(E, L)* The Gospel of Christ
II Cor. 3:4-9 *(R)* Letter and Spirit
Go. Luke 10:23-37 *(R)* Good Samaritan
Luke 18:9-14 *(E, L)* The Pharisee and the Publican

TWELFTH SUNDAY AFTER TRINITY *(E, L;* green), or Thirteenth Sunday
After Pentecost *(R;* white)
Ep. II Cor. 3:4-11 *(E, L)* Letter and Spirit
Gal. 3:16-22 *(R)* The Law and Grace
Go. Mark 7:31-37 *(E, L)* Healing of One Deaf and Dumb
Luke 17:11-19 *(R)* Healing of Ten Lepers

THIRTEENTH SUNDAY AFTER TRINITY *(E, L;* green) or Fourteenth
Sunday After Pentecost *(R;* white)
Ep. Gal. 3:15-22 *(E, L)* The Law and Grace
Gal. 5:16-24 *(R)* Spirit and Flesh
Go. Matt. 6:24-33 *(R)* God and Mammon
Luke 10:23-37 *(E, L)* The Good Samaritan

FOURTEENTH SUNDAY AFTER TRINITY *(E, L;* green), or Fifteenth Sunday
After Pentecost *(R;* white)
Ep. Gal. 5:16-24 *(E, L)* Spirit and Flesh
Gal. 5:26-6:1-10 *(R)* Walk in the Spirit
Go. Luke 7:11-16 *(R)* Raising of the Widow's Son
Luke 17:1-19 *(E, L)* Healing of Ten Lepers

FIFTEENTH SUNDAY AFTER TRINITY *(E, L;* green), or Sixteenth Sunday
After Pentecost *(R;* white)
Ep. Gal. 5:25-6:1-10 *(E, L)* Walk in the Spirit
Eph. 3:13-21 *(R)* Paul's Prayer for the Christians

Go. Matt. 6:24-34 *(E, L)* God and Mammon
  Luke 14:1-11 *(R)* Healing on the Sabbath

SIXTEENTH SUNDAY AFTER TRINITY *(E, L;* green), or Seventeenth Sunday After Pentecost *(R;* white)
Ep. Eph. 3:13-21 *(E, L)* Paul's Prayer for the Christians
  Eph. 4:1-6 *(R)* One Lord, One Faith, One Baptism
Go. Matt. 22:35-46 *(R)* The Great Commandment
  Luke 7:11-17 *(E, L)* Raising of the Widow's Son

SEVENTEENTH SUNDAY AFTER TRINITY *(E, L;* green), or Eighteenth Sunday After Pentecost *(R;* white)
Ep. I Cor. 1:4-6 *(R)* Paul's Thanks for the Christians
  Eph. 4:1-6 *(E, L)* One Lord, One Faith, One Baptism
Go. Matt. 9:1-8 *(R)* Healing One Sick of the Palsy
  Luke 14-1-11 *(E, L)* Healing on the Sabbath

EIGHTEENTH SUNDAY AFTER TRINITY *(E, L;* green), or Nineteenth Sunday After Pentecost *(R;* white)
Ep. I Cor. 1:4-9 *(E, L)* Paul's Thanks for the Christians
  Eph. 4:23-28 *(R)* Renewal in the Spirit
Go. Matt. 22:2-14 *(R)* Parable of the Marriage Feast
  Matt. 22:34-46 *(E, L)* The Great Commandment

NINETEENTH SUNDAY AFTER TRINITY *(E, L* green), or Twentieth Sunday After Pentecost *(R;* white)
Ep. Eph. 4:22-28 *(E, L)* Renewal in the Spirit
  Eph. 5:15-21 *(R)* Redeeming the Time
Go. Matt. 9:1-8 *(E, L)* Healing of One Sick of Palsy
  John 4:46-53 *(R)* Healing of the Ruler's Son

TWENTIETH SUNDAY AFTER TRINITY *(E, L;* green), or Twenty-first Sunday After Pentecost *(R;* white)
Ep. Eph. 5:15-21 *(E, L)* Redeeming the Time
  Eph. 6:10-17 *(R)* Be Strong in the Lord
Go. Matt. 18:23-35 *(R)* Parable of the Talents
  Matt. 22:1-14 *(E, L)* Parable of the Marriage Feast

TWENTY-FIRST SUNDAY AFTER TRINITY *(E, L;* green), or Twenty-second Sunday After Pentecost *(R;* white)
Ep. Eph. 6:10-17 *(E, L)* Be Strong in the Lord
  Phil. 1:6-11 *(R)* Confidence in Christ

Go. Matt. 22:15-21 *(R)* Caesar's Coin
John 4:46-54 *(E, L)* Healing of the Ruler's Son

TWENTY-SECOND SUNDAY AFTER TRINITY *(E, L;* green), or Twenty-third
Sunday After Pentecost *(R;* white)
Ep. Phil. 1:3-11 *(E, L)* Confidence in Christ
Phil. 3:17–4:3 *(R)* Conversation in Heaven
Go. Matt. 9:18-26 *(R)* Jesus the Healer
Matt. 18.23-35 *(E, L)* Parable of the Talents

TWENTY-THIRD SUNDAY AFTER TRINITY *(E, L;* green), or Twenty-fourth
and last Sunday After Pentecost *(R;* white)
Ep. Phil. 3:17-21 *(E, L)* Conversation in Heaven
Col. 1:9-14 *(R)* Paul's Prayer for the Christians
Go. Matt. 22:15-22 *(E, L)* Caesar's Coin
Matt. 24:15-35 *(R)* Of Final Things

TWENTY-FOURTH SUNDAY AFTER TRINITY *(E, L;* green), or Supple-
mentary Mass No. 1 *(R;* white)—same as Sixth Sunday After the
Epiphany
Ep. Col. 1:3-12 *(E)* Inheritance of the Saints
Col. 1:9-14 *(L)* Paul's Prayer for the Christians
I Thess. 1:2-10 *(R)* Fruit of the Gospel
Go. Matt. 9:18-26 *(E, L)* Jesus the Healer
Matt. 13:31-35 *(R)* Parable of the Mustard Seed

TWENTY-FIFTH SUNDAY AFTER TRINITY *(E, L;* green), or Supplementary
Mass No. 2 *(R;* white)—same as Fifth Sunday After the Epiphany.
E also revert to the Sundays after the Epiphany for extra Sundays
After Trinity
Ep. I Thess. 4:13-18 *(L)* Hope of Resurrection
Col. 3-12-17 *(E, R)* Christian Virtues
Go. Matt. 13:24-30 *(E, R)* Tares and Wheat
Matt. 24:15-28 *(L)* Of Final Things

TWENTY-SIXTH SUNDAY AFTER TRINITY *(E, L;* green), or Supplementary
Mass No. 3 *(R;* white)—same as Fourth Sunday After the Epiphany
Ep. II Pet. 3:3-14 *(L)* In the Last Days
or II Thess. 1:3-10 *(L)* The Coming of the Lord
Rom. 13:8-10 *(E, R)* The Powers That Be
Go. Matt. 8:23-27 *(E, R)* Stilling the Storm
Matt. 25:31-46 *(L)* When the Son Shall Come

Twenty-seventh Sunday After Trinity *(E, L;* green), or Supplementary Mass No. 4 *(R;* white)—same as Third Sunday After the Epiphany
Ep. Rom. 12:16-21 *(E, R)* Overcoming Evil with Good
    I Thess. 5:1-11 *(L)* Of Times and Seasons
Go. Matt. 8:1-13 *(E, R)* Cleansing of the Leper
    Matt. 25:1-13 *(L)* Parable of the Ten Virgins

Sunday Next Before Advent *(E, L;* green)

The Episcopalian Book offers this as the final service of the Trinity Season, however many Sundays there may be. It is comparable to the Catholic Twenty-fourth Sunday after Pentecost in having the right of way for the close of the Church Year.

Ep. Jer. 23:5-8 *(E)* The Lord Our Righteousness
Go. John 6:5-14 *(E)* Feeding the Multitudes

CALENDAR OF FIXED DAYS

FIRST QUARTER

JANUARY

The Roman Januarius, added as the beginning month by Numa, honoring Janus, god of opening and shutting and protector of the peace.

In the Christian Year, January falls in Epiphany Season, with missionary emphasis. It also has important commemorations of Christ, Mary, Timothy, and Paul.

Ring out the darkness of the land,
Ring in the Christ that is to be.
—Alfred, Lord Tennyson

1 The civil New Year's Day
1 The Circumcision *(E, R)*
1 *Day of Prayer*
First full week: Universal Week of Prayer *(P)*
5 Epiphany Eve
6 Epiphany
24 Timothy's Day
25 Conversion of Paul

FEBRUARY

The Roman Februarius, added as the last month of the year by Numa, made the second month in 452 B.C. Dedicated to Februus, god of purification. It was shortened to 28 days by the lengthening of July to 31. An extra day is added in leap years.

In the Christian Year, February concurs with Epiphany Season or Pre-Lent. It also has important national celebrations around the birthdays of two presidents, Washington and Lincoln. It is called International Brotherhood Month, and is also given a patriotic emphasis.

Foul weather is no news; hail, rain, and snow
Are now expected, and esteemed no woe;

CALENDAR OF FIXED DAYS

Nay, 'tis an omen bad, the yeomen say,
If Phoebus shows his face the second day.
—The County Almanac, 1676
(quoted in MacDougall's *The Gourmet's Almanac*)

First Sunday: Youth Sunday, or Scout Sunday *(P)*
First full week: Boy Scout Anniversary Week
2   Candlemas; Purification of Mary; Presentation of Christ in the Temple; Greek, Hypapante
12   Abraham Lincoln born—1809
Sunday nearest: Race Relations Sunday *(P)*
14   St. Valentine's Day; Old Candlemas Day—dating from A.D. 270
22   George Washington born—1732
Sunday nearest: Brotherhood Day, or Goodwill Day, with the week following designated Brotherhood Week *(P)*
24   Matthias' Day (in leap years, Feb. 25)
29   Leap Year Day, added in years divisible by 4, except those ending in even hundreds

⟨MARCH⟩

The Roman Martius, first month of the old Roman year, dedicated to Mars, god of war. Although January and February were added early to the calendar, March remained the beginning month until the Gregorian reform.

In the Christian Year it usually concurs with Lent, which may begin as early as February 4 or as late as March 10. It is also the month of spring, with seasonal meaning added to the emphasis of the Church Year.

Easter month, time of hopes and of swallows.
—Helen Gray Cove

17   St. Patrick's Day—dating from A.D. 461

SPRING

Fresh Spring, the herald of love's mighty king,
In whose cote-armour richly are display'd
All sorts of flowers, the which on earth do spring,
In goodly colours gloriously array'd.
—Edmund Spenser

21   First Day of Spring: the Spring Equinox
22   Earliest possible Easter Date
25   The Annunciation: Lady Day

THE STORY OF THE CHRISTIAN YEAR

SECOND QUARTER

——————*⊰{ APRIL }⊱*——————

The Roman Aprilis, from *aperire,* meaning "to open."
In the Christian Year, April concurs with part of Lent, or Eastertide, the latest Easter date being April 25.

> *When proud-pied April, dress'd in all his trim,*
> *Hath put a spirit of youth in everything.*
> —WILLIAM SHAKESPEARE

1	All Fools' Day, or April Fools' Day
13	Thomas Jefferson born—1743
25	John Mark's Day
25	Latest possible Easter date

——————*⊰{ MAY }⊱*——————

The Roman Maius, from Maia, mother of Hercules.
In the Christian Year this month may fall in Eastertide, or Ascensiontide and Whitsuntide.

> *What is so sweet and dear*
> *As a prosperous morn in May,*
> *The confident prime of the day,*
> *And the dauntless youth of the year?*
> —SIR WILLIAM WATSON

1	May Day
1	Philip's and James's Day

First full week: Christian Family Week *(P)* beginning with Child Health Sunday and concluding with the traditional Mother's Day, recently changed to the Festival of the Christian Home

30	Memorial Day, or Decoration Day

Sunday nearest: Memorial Sunday

——————*⊰{ JUNE }⊱*——————

The Roman Junius, dedicated to Juno, consort of Jupiter, Queen of Heaven and goddess of womanhood; also to youth (*junioribus*).
In the Christian Year, June is usually in the beginning of Trinity Season, sometimes also containing Ascensiontide and Whitsuntide. This is the commencement month in public and church schools, and the beginning of the summer season.

> *And what is so rare as a day in June?*
> *Then, if ever, come perfect days.*
> —JAMES RUSSELL LOWELL

CALENDAR OF FIXED DAYS

First Sunday: Christian Unity Sunday *(P)*, and Nature Sunday
Second Sunday: Children's Day; Promotion Day, or Commencement
Sunday

11 Barnabas' Day

Third Sunday: Fathers' Day *(P)*

SUMMER

When as the rye reach to the chin,
And chopcherry, chopcherry ripe within,
Strawberries swimming in the cream,
And schoolboys playing in the stream.
—GEORGE PEELE

21 First Day of Summer
22 Longest Day of the year: Summer Solstice
23 Midsummer Eve, and St. John's Night
24 Midsummer Day, and John the Baptist's Day
29 Peter's Day

THIRD QUARTER

Roman month Julius; Quintilis in the old year, renamed for the Emperor, who was born on the fourth of its ides, and lengthened to 31 days by reducing February.

In the Christian Year, July is in Trinity Season. It is the period of summer religious assemblies, the month of Independence.

July, to whom the Dog-star in her train,
St. James gives oisters, and St. Swithin rain.
—CHURCHILL
(from MacDougall's *The Gourmet's Almanac*)

4 Declaration of Independence; Independence Day; Fourth of
July—1776

Sunday nearest: Independence Sunday

25 St. James's Day
26 St. Anne's Day, honoring grandmother of Jesus

⸨ AUGUST ⸩

The Roman month Augustus, Sextilis in the old year, changed in honor of Emperor Augustus. It is harvest month.

In the Christian Year, August falls in Trinity Season. Harvest festivals may occur in this month, or at any time until late November.

> *It is the Harvest moon! . . .*
> *Gone are the birds that were our summer guests,*
> *With the last sheaves return the laboring wains!*
> —HENRY WADSWORTH LONGFELLOW

6   The Transfiguration *(E, R)*
15   The Assumption *(R)*
24   Bartholomew's Day
Last Sunday: The Festival of Christ the King *(P)*

⸨ SEPTEMBER ⸩

The seventh month of the old Roman, or Martial, year, hence it name.

In the Christian Year, September falls in Trinity Season, and in the *(P)* subseason of Kingdomtide.

> *Season of mists and mellow fruitfulness,*
> *Close bosom-friend of the maturing sun.*
> —JOHN KEATS

First Monday: Labor Day
Sunday nearest: Labor Sunday
14   Holy Cross Day (reference point for the autumn Ember Days)
Wednesday, Friday, and Saturday following: Autumn Ember Days
17   Constitution Day; U. S. Constitution adopted—1787
21   Matthew's Day

AUTUMN

> *Thou comest, Autumn, heralded by the rain*
> *With banners, by great gales incessant fanned.*
> —Author unknown

23   First Day of Autumn: The Equinox
29   Michaelmas Day; St. Michael's and All Angels' Day

226

FOURTH QUARTER

———————⊰{ OCTOBER }⊱———————

The Eighth month of the old Roman, or Martial, year, hence its name.

In the Christian Year, October falls in Trinity Season, and in the *(P)* sub-season of Kingdomtide.

> *When the frost is on the punkin and the fodder's in the shock.*
> —JAMES WHITCOMB RILEY

First Sunday: World Wide Communion Sunday—established 1939 *(P)*
First full week: Religious Education Week—established 1930 *(P)*
Second full week: Week of the Ministry *(P)*
12   Columbus Day, Landing Day, or Discovery Day—1492
18   Luke's Day
28   Simon's and Jude's Day
Last Sunday: Festival of Christ the King *(R)*
31   Halloween, All Hallows' Eve, or Eve of All Saints' Day
31   Reformation Day, commemorating Luther's signing of the Thesis *(P)* 1517
Sunday nearest: Reformation Sunday *(P)*

———————⊰{ NOVEMBER }⊱———————

The ninth month of the old Roman year, hence its name.

In the Christian Year, November falls in Trinity Season, and in the *(P)* sub-season of Kingdomtide. It is Thanksgiving month.

> *Listen . . .*
> *With faint dry sound,*
> *Like steps of passing ghosts,*
> *The leaves, frost crisp'd, break from the trees.*
> —ADELAIDE CRAPSEY

1   All Saints' Day; All Hallowmas, or All Hallows' Day
Sunday nearest: All Saints' Sunday
2   All Souls' Day
Some Sunday: usually designated Loyalty Sunday, Mobilization Sunday, or Stewardship Sunday *(P)*
First full week: Fathers' and Sons' Week *(P)*
First Tuesday: National Election Day
11   Armistice Day
Sunday nearest: Armistice Sunday, World Peace Sunday, or International Good Will Sunday—also Red Cross Sunday; World Government Day

Third Sunday: National Missions in the Sunday Schools Day *(P)*
Third Sunday: Men and Missions Sunday—established 1930 by Laymen's Missionary Movement *(P)*
Last Thursday: National Thanksgiving Day
Sunday nearest: Thanksgiving Sunday
30   Andrews' Day (close of the Christian Year)

──────────*{DECEMBER}*──────────

The tenth month of the old Roman year, hence its name. The month of the Saturnalia and Juvenalis.

In the Christian Year, December is the month of Advent and Christmas, with important fixed days relating to the birth of Christ.

> *When feather'd rain came softly down,*
> *As Jove descending from his tower.*
> —WILLIAM STRODE

 8   Immaculate Conception *(R)*
13   St. Lucy's Day (reference point for the winter Ember days)
Wednesday, Friday, and Saturday following: Winter Ember Days
15   American Bill of Rights Adopted: Bill of Rights Day—1791
21   The Winter Solstice
21   Thomas' Day
21   Landing of the Pilgrims: Forefathers' Day *(P)*—1620

WINTER

> *It was the winter wild*
> *While the heaven-born Child*
> *All meanly wrapped in the rude manger lies.*
> —JOHN MILTON

22   The First Day of Winter
24   Christmas Eve
25   Christmas Day
Sunday nearest: Christmas Sunday

The Christmas Martyrs:
26   Stephens' Day
27   John's Day
28   Holy Innocents' Day
31   New Year's Eve; Watch Night

SELECTED BIBLIOGRAPHY

ARCHER, PETER. *The Christian Calendar and the Gregorian Reform.* New York: Fordham University Press, 1941.

BAINTON, ROLAND. *The Church of Our Fathers.* New York: Charles Scribner's Sons, 1941.

BEDE, THE VENERABLE. *Ecclesiastical History.* New York: E. P. Dutton & Co. (Everyman's Library).

The Book of Common Prayer of the Protestant Episcopal Church. New York: Oxford University Press, 1928.

BUTLER, THE REV. ALBAN. *Lives of the Saints* (abridged, 1887). New York: Benziger Bros.

Chronicles of the Pilgrim Fathers. New York: E. P. Dutton & Co. (Everyman's Library).

CLARKE, JAMES FREEMAN. *Ten Great Religions.* Boston: Houghton Mifflin Co., 1890.

Common Service Book of the Lutheran Church. Philadelphia: Board of Publication of the United Lutheran Church in America, 1919.

COSIN, JOHN; liturgiologist, 1672, works.

DOWDEN JOHN. *The Church Year and Kalendar.* New York: Macmillan Co. (Cambridge Press), 1910.

FAGLEY, FREDERICK L. *A Guide to the Christian Year* (booklet). New York: Commission on Evangelism and Devotional Life (Congregational), 1937.

FISHER, GEORGE PARK. *History of the Christian Church.* New York: Charles Scribner's Sons, 1895.

HAUSMAN, THE REV. BERNARD, S. J. *Learning the Breviary.* New York: Benziger Bros., 1932.

IDLESOHN, ABRAHAM Z. *Ceremonies of Judaism.* Cincinnati: National Federation of Temple Brotherhoods, 1930.

KEBLE, JOHN. *The Christian Year* (in verse), 1827. New York: E. P. Dutton & Co. (Everyman's Library).

229

MacDougall, Allan Ross. *The Gourmet's Almanac.* London: Harmsworth.

Robbins, Howard Chandler. *Preaching the Gospel.* New York: Harper & Bros., 1939.

Roman Catholic Missal, arranged by the Rev. F. X. Lacanse. New York: Benziger Bros., 1939.

A Short Breviary. Collegeville, Minn.: Liturgical Press, 1942.

Staley, Vernon. *The Liturgical Year.* London: A. R. Mowbray & Co., 1907.

———. *The Seasons, Fasts and Festivals of the Christian Year* (English Churchmen's Library). London: A. R. Mowbray & Co., 1910.

Walker Williston. *A History of the Christian Church.* New York: Charles Scribner's Sons, 1918.

Williams, Charles. *The New Christian Year.* New York: Oxford University Press, 1941.

Wilson, Frank E. *An Outline of the Christian Year* (booklet). New York: Morehouse-Goreham Co., 1941.

INDEX

Ab, 41
  Fast of, 54
Ab urbe condita, 29
Adar, 41, 50
Advent, 26, 77, 78, 93, 95, 96, 97, 100,
    129, 140, 189, 190, 221
  mid-Advent, 205
  season, 205
  Sunday next before, 153
  Sundays of, 96, 97, 205
Agnes', St., Eve, 154
Alb Sunday, 210
All Angels' Day, 127, 226
All Fools' Day, 224
All Hallowmas, 227
All Hallows' Day, and Eve, 227
All Saints' Day, and Eve, 117, 154, 180,
    190, 227
All Saints' Sunday, 227
All Souls' Day, 117, 190, 227
All the Sundays in the Year, 191, 205-21
American Bill of Rights Day, 175, 227
American month, 15
Andrews' St., Day, 95, 97, 227
Anne's, St., Day, 115, 225
Anno Domini, 38, 106, 201
Annunciation Day, 90, 115, 140, 223
Ante Christum, 38, 106
Anthony's, St., Day, 116, 174
Apokreos Sunday, 208
Apostles' days (including N. T.
    saints), 137, 140
  All Saints, 227
  Andrew, 227
  Barnabas, 154, 225
  Bartholomew, 226
  Innocents, 225
  James, 224, 225
  John, the Evangelist, 228
  John the Baptist, 225
  Jude, 226
  Luke, 226

  Mark, 224
  Matthew, 226
  Matthias, 223
  Paul, 222
  Peter, 225
  Philip, 224
  Simon, 226
  Stephen, 228
  Thomas, 228
April, 57, 104, 224
April Fools' Day, 224
Aprilis, 57, 62, 224
Arbor Day, 49
Armistice Day, 175, 227
Armistice Sunday, 227
Ascension Day, 37, 79, 84, 90, 93, 97,
    140, 190, 214
  Monday, Tuesday, Wednesday be-
    fore, 121
  Sunday after, 214
Ascension of Our Lord, 214
Ascension Sunday, 85
Ascensiontide, 97, 99, 214
Ash Wednesday, 91, 98, 153, 209
  Wednesday, Friday, Saturday after, 122
Ass, Feast of the, 128
Assumption, Feast of the, 115, 226
Atonement, Feast of the, 16, 47
August, 57, 59, 115, 126, 217, 226
Augustine of England, 110
Augustine of Hippo, 108, 174
Augustus, 48, 64, 225
Autumn, 15, 40, 226
  Ember days, 226

Baptism, Feast of the, of Christ, 85,
    114, 207
Barnabas', St., Day (Barnaby Bright),
    154, 225
Bartholomew's, St., Day, 226
Beating of the bounds, 121, 153, 214
Before Christ, 38

231

Before the common era, 38
Bible, Universal, Sunday, 48, 174, 181, 205
Bill of Rights Day, 175, 228
Birthday of Christ, 87, 206
Birthday of the Church, 70, 82, 215
Black Mass, 128
Black Sunday, 210
Blessed Virgin Mary; see Mary
Book Week, 175
Booths, Feast of, 47
Boy Scout Anniversary Week, 223
Branches, Sunday of, 210
Brotherhood Day, and Week, 222, 223
Brumaire, 171

Calendar
  Christian, 37-38, 91, 102, 103
  of fixed days, 222-28
  French, 170
  general, 15-17, 34, 74, 100, 104, 177
  Jewish, 36-37, 40
  reform, 184-86
  Roman, 56
Calends, 58
Calvin, 175
Candlemas, 115, 223
  old, 223
Cantate Sunday, 213
Care Sunday, 210
Carnival, 77, 209
Cecilia's, St., Day, 119, 121
Centuries, 27
Chamishah, 49
Chanukah, 48, 49
Chechwan, 41
Child Health Sunday, 224
Children's Day, 174, 175, 225
Christ; see Jesus
Christ the King, Festival of, 126, 174, 190, 218, 225, 226
Christian Calendar, 37-38, 91, 102, 103
Christian Era, 28, 30, 31, 59, 129
Christian Family Week, 175, 224
Christian Home, Festival of the, 175, 224
Christian Unity Sunday, 225
Christian Year, 8, 16, 26, 27, 37, 39, 56, 68, 69, 74-81, 95-97, 99, 102, 104, 107, 118-22, 127, 133, 134, 138, 139, 141, 143, 148, 153, 154, 156, 158, 160,

163, 169, 171, 173, 176-78, 180-85, 187-89, 191, 192, 195-98, 200
Christmas, 27, 37, 40, 64, 79, 80, 83, 87-90, 98, 101, 114, 140, 159, 160, 169, 173, 206, 228
  Eve, 95, 228
  martyrs, 228
  Old, 85, 207
  Sunday, 206
  Sunday before, 205
  -tide, 78, 97, 99, 113, 206, 228
  White, 174
Christ's Mass, 88
Church, Birthday of the, 70, 215
Church Year, 19, 82, 83, 87, 95, 111, 121, 122, 124, 129, 131, 137, 140, 148, 151, 173, 176, 178, 180, 184, 187, 189, 191, 192, 194, 197, 198, 205
Circumcision, Feast of the, 90, 99, 101, 126, 140, 206, 222
Claustra, tempora, 98
Clean Lent, 209
Clericos laicos, 131, 139
Collop Monday, 153, 209
Colors, ecclesiastical, 99, 205-21
Columbus Day, 175, 227
Commencement Sunday, 225
Common era, 38
Communion, 72, 81, 85, 128, 129, 211
  World Wide, Sunday, 174, 226
Constitution, U. S., 15, 175, 226
Copernican astronomy, 36, 38, 141
Corpus Christi Day, 99, 100, 126, 129, 216
  Friday after octave of, 216
  Sunday within octave of, 216
Cotsworth calendar, 185
Creation, 28, 31, 42, 44, 72, 90, 95, 97
Cycles, 28

Daughters' Day, Mothers' and, 175
Day, the, 70, 73, 76, 173
Daylight-saving time, 186
Decade, the, 27
Decades, 170
December, 29, 57, 62, 64, 65, 87, 89, 90, 116, 122, 126, 167, 172, 185, 227-28
Decision Day, 174
Decoration Day, 224
Dedication, Feast of, 48
Discovery Day, 227

Dolors, Feast of the Seven, of the B. V. M., 115, 210

Easter, 27, 37, 52, 58, 70, 78-85, 88-94, 96-98, 102-104, 111, 113, 118, 127, 140, 151, 153, 158-60, 169, 173, 185, 186, 190
  Act, 186
  days after, 213
  days before, 211
  earliest, 223
  Even, 91, 93, 212
  latest, 224
  Sunday, Feast of, 212
  -tide, 93, 97, 99, 212
  weekly, 73
Ecclesiastical Year, 9, 39, 71, 89, 120, 122, 123, 127, 130, 132, 137, 147, 149, 153, 160, 165, 172, 187, 197, 200, 201
Election, National, Day, 227
Elul, 41
Ember days, and weeks, 24, 121-22, 126
  autumn, 226
  spring, 209
  summer, 215
  winter, 228
Epiphany, 26, 37, 79, 85-87, 89, 96-99, 126, 140, 207, 222
  Eve, 222
  season, 93, 222
  Sundays after, 96, 207, 208
Equinox,
  autumnal, 25, 226
  spring, 25, 90, 223
Eras, 27 ff.
Espousal, Feast of the, of the B. V. M., 115
Eternity, 23
Ethanim, 48
Eucharist, 69, 71, 139
Evangelists; see Apostles
Exaltation of the Holy Cross, 126
Exaudi Sunday, 214
Expectation Sunday, 85, 214

Family, Christian, Week, 175, 224
Fast of the Four Seasons, 122
Fast of Gedalia, 46
Fasts and fasting, 73, 77, 92, 122, 171, 198
Fat Tuesday, 209

Fathers' Day, 175, 225
  and Sons' Day, and Week, 175, 227
Feasts and feasting, 17, 76, 77, 81, 82, 92, 98, 99, 140, 152-54, 171, 173, 201
Februarius, 57, 58, 61, 222
February, 105, 115, 126, 222
Festivals; see Feasts
First day, 68, 70, 71, 160
First half year, 96, 97, 205-15
First month, 59, 222
First quarter, 222-23
First Sunday after Easter, 213
First Sunday after Epiphany, 207
Fixed days, calendar of, 222-28
Flag Day, 175
Floréal, 171
Fools, Feast of, 102, 128
Forefathers' Day, 167, 174, 228
Forty days, great, 209-12
Fourth of July, 225
Franciade, 171
Francis of Assisi, 174
Friday, 45, 91, 98, 122, 215, 226, 227
  after Corpus Christi, 216
  in Holy Week (Good Friday), 47, 97, 100, 190, 209, 212
  in Passion Week, 115, 210
Frimaire, 171
Fructidor, 171

Gabriel, St., of the Sorrowful Mother, 115
Games, 65, 72, 158
Gang days, and week, 154, 214
Gaudete Sunday, 205
Gedaliah, Fast of, 46
Gentlemen's days, 171
Germinal, 171
God's Sunday, 212
Good Friday, 47, 97, 100, 190, 209, 212
Good Will Sunday, 175, 223, 227
Great forty days, 209-12
Great Sabbath, 212
Great Sunday, 212
Great Week, 93, 210
Gregorian calendar, 31, 38, 39, 58, 141, 184, 186

Habdalah, 45
Haggadah, 52
Halloween, 154, 180, 227

Harvest Festival, 48, 169, 225
Hegira, 31
Heroes of Peace Day, 181
Holy apostles; *see* Apostles' days
Holy Communion; *see* Communion
Holy Cross Day, 122, 126, 226
Holy Day, 40, 69, 73, 117
Holy Family, Feast of the, 207
Holy Innocents' Day, 105, 228
Holy name; *see* Jesus *and* Mary *and* Name, holy
Holy Saturday, 212
Holy Sunday, 212
Holy Thursday, 84, 121, 214
Holy Trinity, Festival of the, 215
Holy Week, 91, 92, 93, 97, 210-12
  special days in, 211-12
Home, Festival of the Christian, 175, 224
Hypapante, 223

Ides, 58
Immaculate Conception, Feast of the, 115, 116, 228
Incarnation, 31, 95, 114, 206
Independence Day, and Sunday, 15, 175, 225
Indiction, 29
Intercalary month, 41, 58
International Brotherhood Day, Week, and Month, 222, 223
International Good Will Sunday, 227
Interrace Sunday, 175, 223
Invention of the Cross, 126
Invocavit Sunday, 209
Iyyar, 41

James the Greater, 225
James's Day, Philip's and, 224
Januarius, 57, 60, 126, 222
January, 17, 58, 87, 115, 222
Jefferson, Thomas, 175, 224
Jerusalem Sunday, 210
Jesus, 126, 140
  Christ the King, Festival of, 218, 226, 227
  circumcision of, 206, 222
  days honoring, 126
  Epiphany, 207-8, 222
  Holy Name of, Feast of the, 206, 222
  nativity of, 206, 228

presentation of, 223
transfiguration of, 208, 226
Jewish calendar, 36, 40, 41, 44, 45, 48, 56, 120
Jewish ceremonial year, 42, 43, 70, 89, 133, 194
Jewish era, 42
Jewish New Year, 16, 40, 46, 47
Jewish Thanksgiving, 47
John the Baptist's Day, and Night, 105, 140, 154, 225
John, St., the Divine's, Day, 105, 228
Jubilate Sunday, 213
Jubilee, year of, 43, 44, 49
Jude's and Simon's Day, 227
Judica Sunday, 210
Julian calendar, 37-39, 58, 59, 88, 141
Julius, 63, 225
July, 57, 58, 115, 126, 225
June, 57, 185, 224
Junius, 57, 63, 224

Kingdomtide, 16, 198, 217, 225
Kislew, 41, 48

Labor Day, and Sunday, 15, 175, 226
Lady Day, 223
Laetare Sunday, 210
Lammas Day, 154
Landing Day, 228
Lawrence's, St., Day, 140
Leap year, 38, 58
  Day, 185, 223
Lent, 26, 53, 77, 78, 91-93, 97, 100, 153, 181, 190, 209, 223
  Clean, 209
  first day of, 209
  mid-Lent, 210
  pre-Lent, 78, 93, 208, 222
  season, 93, 209
  Sundays before, 208
  Sundays in, 92, 209-10
  winter, 95, 205
Lights, Feast of, 48, 49
Lincoln, Abraham, 175, 223
Loaf Mass, 154
Lord's Day, 70, 71, 80, 141, 157, 160
  Alliance, 159, 213
Lord's Supper, 40, 68, 69, 71, 72
Lost Sunday, 208
Lots, Feast of, 50

Low Sunday, and Week, 153, 213
Loyalty Sunday, 227
Lucy's, St., Day, 122, 154, 228
Luke's Day, 227
Lunar year, 36
Luther, Martin, 139, 174, 227

Maius, 57, 63, 224
Mamertus, Bishop, 214
Manifestation of Christ, 207
March, 57-59, 90, 104, 115, 223
Mardi gras (Shrove Tuesday), 153
Mariology, 115
Mark's, John, Day, 224
Martial year, 15, 57
Martin, St., of Tours' Day, 119
Martinmas, 96
Martius, 57, 62, 223
Martyrs and martyrology, 38, 100, 102,
    105, 113, 115, 117, 118
  Christmas martyrs, 228
Mary, 90, 114, 115, 118, 125, 137, 190
  Anne's, St., Day, 225
  annunciation of, 115, 223
  assumption of, 115, 225
  days honoring, 114-16
  espousal of, 115
  holy name of, 115
  immaculate conception of, 46, 227
  maternity of, 116
  nativity of 115
  purification of, 45, 223
  rosary, 116
  St. Gabriel of Sorrowful Mother, 115
  seven dolors of, 115, 210
  visitation of, 140
Maternity, Feast of the, of the B. V.
    M., 116
Matthew's Day, 226
Matthias' Day, 223
Maunday Thursday, and Vigil of, 81,
    184, 211
May, 57, 58, 63, 126, 154, 224
  Day, 224
Memorial days, 65, 175, 224
  Sunday, 224
Men and Missions Sunday, 174, 227
Mercedonius, 57
Messidor, 171
Michael's, St., and All Angels' Day
    (also Michaelmas), 127, 140, 226
Mid-Advent, 205

Mid-Lent, 210
Midsummer Day, Eve, and Night, 154,
    225
Ministry, Week of the, 174, 227
Miracle plays, 127
Misericordias domini Sunday, 213
Missionary Day, 207
Missions Sunday, 174, 207
  in the Sunday schools, 174, 227
Mobilization Sunday, 227
Monday, 121, 214
  after Easter, 213
  before Easter (in Holy Week), 211
  Shrove, 153, 209
  in Whitsunweek, 215
Month, 58, 73, 146, 161
Morality plays, 127
Mothering Sunday, 210
Mothers' Day (and Daughters'), 175,
    224
Myrrhophori Sunday, 213
Mystery plays, 127

Name, holy, of Jesus, 206
  of Mary, 115
National Election Day, 227
National Missions in Sunday Schools
    Day, 174, 227
Nativity, Feast of the
  of Jesus, 85, 88, 90, 126, 190, 206
  of Mary, 115
Nature Sunday, 175, 225
New style calendar, 38
New Sunday, 210
New Week, 212
New Year, 17, 46, 58, 95, 206, 222
  Christian, 97, 222
  Eve, 228
  Jewish, 16, 40, 46, 47
  Roman, 90
Nicholas', St., Day, 89
Nissan, 40, 41, 51, 104
Nivôse, 171
Nones, 58
November, 57, 64, 95, 96, 117, 227
Nundinae, 58

Octave, 23
Octavus Domini, 206
October, 31, 38, 41, 46, 57, 58, 63, 64,
    116, 126, 172, 226
Oculi Sunday, 210

Old Christmas, 85, 207
Old New Year, 62
Old Roman calendar, 37, 57
Old style calendar, 38, 58
Olympiads, 29
O Sapientia, 126, 129

Palm Sunday, 91, 93, 97, 210
Palmarum, 210
Pan American Day, 175
Pascha, 79, 80, 92, 93
  Rosatum, 215
Passion Hours, 212
Passion Play, 128
Passion Sunday, 93, 210
Passiontide, 93, 210
Passion Week, 93, 210
  Friday in, 210
Passover, 28, 37, 40, 43, 51-53, 69, 70, 72, 79, 82, 83, 89, 194
Patrick's, St., Day, 110, 143, 223
Patron saints, 118
Paul, conversion of, 105, 222
Pentecost
  Christian, 30, 53, 71, 79, 81-85, 91, 94, 97, 122, 181, 190, 215
  festival of, 215
  Jewish, 30, 37, 43, 53, 70, 82
  season, 93, 214-15
  Sundays after, 83, 93, 94, 117, 215-21
  supplementary masses after, 220-21
  Perambulation of parish, 121, 153, 214
Persian period, 42
Pesach, 51
Peter's Day, 225
Philips' and James's Day, 224
Pilgrimages, 139
Pluviôse, 171
Poetry Week, 175
Prairial, 171
Prayer
  World Day of, 174, 222
  Universal Week of, 222
Precious Blood, Feast of the, 126
Pre-Lent, 93, 97, 100, 208
Preparation, days of, 91
Presentation of Christ in the Temple, 126, 223
Promotion Day, 225
Prophetic Week, 43
Ptolemaic astronomy, 36, 38, 141

Purification, Feast of, 115, 140, 222
Purim, Feast of, 50, 51

Quadragesima Sunday, and Season, 92, 209
Quadrenia, 27
Quarter, 1st, 222; 2nd, 224; 3rd, 225; 4th, 226
Quasi Modo Geniti Sunday, 213
Quatuor tempora, 122, 209
Quinquagesima Sunday, 93, 208
Quintilis, 57, 63, 225

Race Relations Sunday, 223
Red Cross Day, and Sunday, 175, 223
Reform calendar, 184-186
Reformation Day, and Sunday, 174, 227
Refreshment Sunday, 210
Rejoicing of the Law, 48
Religious Education Week, 174, 227
Reminiscere Sunday, 209
Renewal Sunday, 213
Resurrection, Feast of the, 71, 212
Rogate Sunday, 213
Roch's, St., Day, 154
Rogation days, and weeks, 121, 153, 154, 213-14
Roman calendar, 57
Roman celebrations, 57-66
Roman holiday, 60
Roman year, 56, 59, 60
Rorate Sunday, 205
Rosary, Most Holy, 116
Rose Sunday, 210
Roses, Feast of, 215
Rosh Hashana, 46
Rural Life Sunday, 175, 214

Sabbath, 22, 37, 43-45, 69-72, 91, 152, 156-59
Sabbatical year, 43-44
Sabo, 43
Sacred Heart, Feast of the, 126, 216
Saints, and saints' days, 67, 89, 100, 104, 111, 113, 114, 116, 117, 120, 122, 137, 144, 147, 151, 156, 174, 182, 184, 199, 200
Sallow Sunday, 210
Sans-culottides, 171
Santa Claus, 89
Sapientia, O, 126, 129

INDEX

Saturday, 97, 122, 185, 186, 209, 215, 226, 227
in Holy Week (Holy Sunday), 212
Saturnalia, 17, 62, 64, 102, 128
Scout, Boy, Sunday, and Week, 223
Seasons, 24, 26, 58, 76, 91, 96, 98, 120, 122, 140, 147, 154, 159, 173, 175, 197, 201
Advent, 205
Ascensiontide, 214
autumn, 226-27
Christmastide, 206
Eastertide, 212-14
Epiphany, 207-8
Kingdomtide, 217-21
Lent, 209-10
Passiontide, 210-12
pre-Lent, 208-9
spring, 223-24
summer, 224-26
Trinity, 215-21
Whitsuntide, 214-15
winter, 228
Second First Sunday, 213
Second half year, 16, 93, 94, 96, 97, 215
Second quarter, 224
Seder, service of, 52
Sefirah Lag Boamer, 53
Seminary Day, 174
September, 15, 46, 57, 59, 64, 115, 122, 126, 172, 226
Septuagesima Sunday, and season, 58, 80, 93, 208
Seven Dolors, Feast of the, 115, 210
Seven Last Words, 212
Seven weeks of years, 43
Sexagesima Sunday, 93, 208
Sextilis, 57, 59, 64, 225
Shabuoth, 53
Shebat, 41, 49
Shepherd Sunday, 213
Shore Thursday, 211
Shows, 66
Shrove days
Monday, 209
Shrovetide, 153, 209
Sunday, 209
Tuesday, 153, 209
Simchath Torah, 48
Simnel Sunday, 210
Simon's and Jude's Day, 227
Siwan, 41, 53

Solar year, 36
Solstice
summer, 25, 225
winter, 25, 87, 90, 227
Spring, 25, 51, 67, 79, 81, 89, 90, 92, 104, 209, 223
first day of, 223
Spy Wednesday, 211
Stations, 98
Stephen's Day, 105, 228
Stewardship Sunday, 174, 227

Stir Up Sunday, 153
Succoth, 47, 48
Summer, 75, 225-26
Ember days, 215
first day of (solstice), 25, 225
Sunday, 37, 70-72, 74, 80, 82, 85, 92-94, 98, 137, 153, 155, 157-59, 173, 186
all the, in the year, 205-21
Great, 212
Holy, 212
Shrove, 209
Sunday Schools, Missions in the, Day, 174, 227
Swiss plan, 185

Tabernacles, Feast of, 16, 43, 47
Tammuz, Fast of, and month, 41, 53
Tebeth, Fast of, and month, 41, 49
Temperance Sunday, 175
Tempora claustra, 98
Tempora, quatuor, 122, 209
Tenebrae, service of, 184, 211
Themes, of the year halves, 205, 214-15
Theresa's, St., Day, 174
Thanksgiving, 39, 47, 154, 166, 169, 174, 175, 227
Sunday, 227
Theological Seminary Day, 174
Theophany, 86, 207
Three Kings, Feast of the, 207
Thermidor, 171
Third quarter, 225-26
Thomas' Day, 228
Three Kings, Feast of the, 207
Thursday, 81, 84, 184
Holy, 84
in Holy Week, (Maundy), 211
Shore, 211
Time, times, and time sense, 16, 17, 19, 27, 34, 73, 89, 138, 159, 166, 178, 216
Timothy's Day, 222

Tish'a Be'ab, 53
Tishre, 40, 41, 46, 47, 48
Tradition Sunday, 210
Transfiguration, Feast of, 126, 208, 226
Trinity
  Feast of, and season, 16, 80, 94, 100
    140, 189, 215-21, 224
  Sundays after, 93, 94, 216-21
  Thursday after, 216
Trumpets, Feast of, 46
Tuesday, 23, 121, 214
  before Easter (in Holy Week), 211
  in Easter Week, 213
  Shrove, 209
  in Whitsunweek, 215
Twelfth Day, and Night, 87, 154, 207

Unity, Christian, Sunday, 225
Universal Bible Sunday, 48, 174, 181, 205
Universal Week of Prayer, 174, 222
Unleavened Bread, Feast of, 51

Valentine's, St., Day, 154, 223
Vedar, 41
Vendémiaire, 171
Ventôse, 171
Vigil of Easter Day, 212
Vigil of Maundy Thursday, 211
Visitation, Feast of the, 140
Vocation Day, 174, 213

Washington, George, 175, 223
Watch Night, 228
Wednesday, 23, 98, 121, 122, 209, 214,
    215, 226, 227
  Ash, 92, 153, 209
  before Easter, 211

Week, and weeks, 21, 23, 43, 173
  Christian Family, 175
  Feast of, 53
  Holy (Great), 92-93, 210-12
  Low, 213
  of the ministry, 174, 227
  New, 212
  of Prayer, 174, 222
  Religious Education, 174, 227
  of weeks, 43
  of years, 43
White Christmas, 174
  Sunday, 82, 213, 215
Whitsunday, and Whitsuntide, 82, 83,
    93, 94, 100, 140, 190, 214, 215
  Monday, Tuesday, in, 215
Winter, 67, 88, 89, 228
Ember days, 228
  Lent, 95
  solstice, 25, 87, 90, 228
World calendar, 185, 186
World Day of Prayer, 174, 209
World Government Day, 227
World holidays, 185
World Peace Sunday, 227
World Temperance Sunday, 175
World-wide Communion Sunday, 174,
    226

Year, 26, 27, 73, 76
Year-end day, 185
Year halves, themes of the, 205, 214-15
Year of our Lord, 38, 106, 201
Yom Kippur, 46, 47
Youth Day, and Sunday, 174, 175, 213,
    223